Residential Lettings

Tessa Shepperson

Residential Lettings
by Tessa Shepperson

1st edition 2000
   Reprinted 2001
2nd edition 2002
3rd edition 2003
   Reprinted 2003
4th edition 2004
5th edition 2005

© 2005 Lawpack Publishing

Lawpack Publishing Limited
76–89 Alscot Road
London SE1 3AW

www.lawpack.co.uk

The right of Tessa Shepperson to be identified as the author of this work has been asserted by her in accordance with the Copyright, Designs and Patents Act 1988.

The contents of this book have been approved under Scottish law by Neill Clerk & Murray, Solicitors.

ISBN: 1 904053 90 4

Exclusion of Liability and Disclaimer

Contents

Important facts   vii
About the author   viii
Foreword   ix
Introduction   xi

1 The legal framework   1
Licences and tenancies   2
   Tenancies   4
   Licences   6
   Lettings which can be either a tenancy or a licence   6
Resident landlords   7
New tenancies today   8
Other legal matters landlords need to know   9
   Fixed-term and periodic tenancies   9
   Section 20 notices   10
   Guarantees   10
   Joint and several liability   11
   Letting your own home   11
   Premiums   12
   Succession rights   12
   Eviction of tenants and eviction notices   12
The winds of change ...   13

2 Initial considerations   15
'Location, location, location'   16
Other considerations   17
   What is your intended type of tenant?   17
   Building or other work   17
   Fixtures and fittings/furniture   18
   The availability of grants   18
   Furnished or unfurnished?   19
   Achievable rent/financial considerations   19

Tenant default   19
Buy-to-let   20
   Buying properties with existing tenants   21
Houses in multiple occupation   22
Local authority assistance   25
Landlords' associations   26

3 Preparation of the property   29
Permission for letting   29
Planning permission   29
Renovations and repairs   30
   Building regulations   32
   Heating   32
   Condensation   32
Gas Regulations   33
   The Gas Safety (Installation and Use) Regulations 1998   33
Electricity   35
Fire safety   35
Water   37
Fitting out the property   37
Product safety regulations   38
   Furniture and furnishings   38
   Electrical equipment   38
   The General Product Safety Regulations   39
   ... and finally   39
Insurance   40
Rent   42
Accreditation   43

4 Finding a tenant   45
Letting agents   45
Advertising for tenants   48
The Property Misdescriptions Act 1991   49
The paramount importance of a good tenant   49
   References   51
   Credit reference agencies   51
   'Gut' feeling   52
Housing Benefit tenants   55
   Housing Benefit claw-back   57

Local Housing Allowance 58
Generally 59
The Rent Service and the assessment of rent for
    Housing Benefit 59
Housing Benefit valuations 60

5 The agreement 63
Why and when is it necessary? 63
The Unfair Terms in Consumer Contracts Regulations 1999 64
Individual terms you will need in the agreement 66
    Essential terms 66
    Other important terms 69
Obtaining tenancy agreements 82
Housing law reform 83

6 During the tenancy 87
The covenant of quiet enjoyment 87
Rent matters 88
    The rent book 88
    Collecting rent 89
    Increasing the rent 89
    Challenges to the rent – the Rent Assessment Committee 92
Repairing duties/access 94
    HMO properties 96
Housing Benefit 97
New tenancy agreements 97
Tax considerations 98
    Income Tax 99
    Capital Gains Tax 99
    VAT 100

7 Problem tenants 101
Take action quickly 101
Landlord's duty to other tenants 101
Gas safety 102
Harassment legislation 103
Evicting tenants 105
    Grounds for possession 106
    Notices 107

Possession proceedings 109
Evicting Rent Act tenants 113
Common law tenancies 113
Squatters and licensees 114
Enforcement of possession orders 114
Excluded tenancies or licences 115
Money claims 115

8 At the end of a tenancy 119
When does the tenancy end? 119
Handover procedure 121
Tenant's property left behind 123
Death of a tenant 124
After the tenant has gone 125
Utilities 125
Post 125

Appendix 127
Index 131

Important facts

This book contains the information and instructions for landlords letting residential properties. This book is for use in England & Wales and in Scotland. It is not intended for use in Northern Ireland.

The information it contains has been carefully compiled from professional sources, but its accuracy is not guaranteed, as laws and regulations may change or be subject to differing interpretations. The law is stated as at 1 March 2005.

Neither this nor any other publication can take the place of a solicitor on important legal matters. As with any legal matter, common sense should determine whether you need the assistance of a solicitor rather than rely solely on the information and forms in this book.

We strongly urge you to consult a solicitor if:

- substantial amounts of money are involved;
- you do not understand the instructions or are uncertain how to complete and use a form correctly;
- what you want to do is not precisely covered by this book;
- trusts or business interests are involved.

About the author

Tessa Shepperson is a solicitor in private practice. She qualified in 1990, and set up her own legal practice, TJ Shepperson, in 1994. Tessa specialises in residential landlord and tenant work and is now concentrating on legal work for private residential landlords. She offers legal services for landlords from her specialist site, Landlord-Law Online (www.landlordlaw.co.uk). Tessa lives in Norwich with her husband and son.

Foreword

As stated in the Introduction to this book, being a residential landlord is not easy, and this has spawned the publication of books and guides that vary in quality, all of which are intended to help landlords. With this in mind, we were apprehensive when asked to review yet another 'practical guide for new and experienced landlords'.

The National Federation of Residential Landlords (NFRL) represents, at a national level, the interests of small, private landlords throughout the country. It is important that they are well-informed as, together, these landlords form the major part of the private rented sector. The NFRL has in its membership virtually all landlords' associations in the country, and it is through this network of 50 landlords' associations, some with many branches, that landlords are represented at local level.

The NFRL relies on these associations to convey information on letting to individual landlords and any publication that assists local associations to carry out this task is welcome. However, many of these publications are confusing, only providing part of the picture or even are sometimes inaccurate.

It was therefore refreshing to discover this clear and balanced publication. Good information raises standards. In doing so, it not only helps tenants but also makes managing residential lettings easier and more profitable. *Residential Lettings* really is a useful companion for landlords new to letting, while experienced landlords who need to check their knowledge will profit from the information it contains.

The NFRL has no hesitation in recommending this publication to landlords; *Residential Lettings* amounts to a management tool that no landlord should be without.

National Federation of Residential Landlords

Introduction

Being a landlord is not as easy as it may appear. It involves a lot of work, yet the general perception of landlords is that they have an easy life getting 'money for nothing'. It is important that landlords realise the extent of the obligations that they are taking on and are aware of their legal responsibilities. Landlords are subject to a plethora of regulations that are regularly amended or added to. Usually they involve penalties for non-compliance. These regulations are intended to protect the tenant; however, they can also protect the landlord to a certain extent because if he complies with them he will have a good defence to any claims that may be made against him by the tenant. Also good-quality properties are more likely to attract good-quality tenants – the 'holy grail' of landlords. The landlord with a good tenant has far, far fewer problems than the landlord with a bad tenant.

This book is intended mainly to be a practical guide for new landlords of short-term residential tenancies, although it will, I hope, be useful to experienced landlords and may also be of interest to tenants. After some initial legal explanation (chapter 2), it aims first to guide you through the things that you should be considering before letting a property, and to help you through the process of getting the property ready for letting, finding a tenant, and making the agreement with the tenant. It then goes on to discuss what happens during a tenancy and what you can do if you have problem tenants. Finally, there is some discussion about what happens, or should happen, at the end of a tenancy.

This book is intended to be a general guide only. If you have any special or unusual problem, you should not rely solely on this book, but should seek independent legal advice. Up-to-date information can also be found on my website Landlord-Law Online, at www.landlordlaw.co.uk.

Acknowledgements

It has been great fun writing this book, and my first thanks should go to my editor, Jamie Ross, for giving me the opportunity to write it.

Part of my research has been talking to landlords and to professionals in relevant fields. I am very grateful to all of them for giving up their time, and this book would not have been possible without them. Any remaining mistakes, however, are mine.

I am particularly indebted to Mike Stimpson and John Stather of the National Federation of Residential Landlords and to Nigel Stringer, all of whom kindly read the manuscript. My grateful thanks also go to all of the following (in no particular order): Colin Lawrence FCIH – Area Manager for Cambridgeshire, Suffolk & Norfolk Rent Service; Bruce Edgington, Solicitor – President, and David Brown FRICS MCIArb – Vice President, Chilterns, Thames & Eastern Rent Assessment Panel; David Bush FRICS – Bush Property Management Ltd; Malcolm Turton – Eastern Landlords Association and National Federation of Residential Landlords; Mike Edmunds – Housing Advisor, Norwich Advice Services; John Spencer – Principal Housing Improvement Officer, Norwich City Council; Paul E Carter – HM Principal Inspector of Health & Safety, Health & Safety Executive, Norwich; Beverley Whittaker – Benefits Manager, Revenue Service, Norwich City Council; David Beard and Jonathan Peddle – Norfolk Trading Standards; Robert Graver – Director, Alan Boswell Insurance Brokers Ltd; Nick Saffell FRICS – Partner, Brown & Co; Sally Baits – Solicitor, Norwich City Council; Ian MacLeod M.I.Fire.E – Fire Safety Officer, Norfolk Fire Service.

I am also indebted to all the various landlords I have known and acted for over the years, and to the landlords in the Eastern Landlords Association who have chatted to me at meetings about their problems and experiences as landlords. Many thanks also to my husband Graeme and my mother for their help and encouragement while I was writing this book.

Tessa Shepperson

CHAPTER 1

The legal framework

It is important that landlords understand the basic legal framework and the various types of lettings that exist. This is because these differences have important ramifications and implications for the rights of landlords and tenants. I will be discussing these in more detail at various stages later in the book.

Housing and the rights of tenants have always been important political issues and there has been a series of Acts of Parliament on housing matters over the years. This makes the whole subject legally rather complex. A landlord's or tenant's rights will, to a large extent, depend upon the Act of Parliament which regulates the tenancy, which in turn depends upon the date when the tenancy originally started. As this book is aimed at new landlords, I will primarily consider the legal situation for a new tenancy (as opposed to a new agreement for an existing tenancy) created after January 2000. However, most of the general points discussed will still be very relevant for older tenancies and landlords with existing tenants. I will try to indicate in the text where any differences occur to assist landlords of older tenancies.

This book can be read in relation to lettings in England & Wales and in Scotland; any differences in law are highlighted.

Note

This book deals only with short-term lettings (i.e. for less than seven years). Long-term leases, normally purchased with a premium, are not covered.

Licences and tenancies

In landlord and tenant law generally, there is a fundamental difference between a licence and a tenancy. A licence is where the owner of the property gives someone permission to occupy it. A tenancy is where the tenant acquires a 'legal interest' in the property. This 'legal interest', i.e. the tenancy/lease, is more than just permission to live in the property for a while, it is something that is capable of being bought and sold, and can pass to another person after the initial tenant dies.

With a tenancy, one way of looking at it is to consider that the landlord 'sells' the property to the tenant for a period of time in exchange for rent and the right for the landlord to get the property back after the tenancy ends (what lawyers call the 'reversion'). So, in many respects, while the tenancy is in existence it is the tenant who 'owns' the property, not the landlord.

Property law being what it is, things are not as simple as that. The various Acts of Parliament which regulate short-term lettings have incorporated a number of rights and obligations into tenancies (and to a much lesser extent, licences) which the landlord is unable to exclude from the letting, however much he may want to (and even if the licensee/tenant agrees to him being excluded).

One of the most important rights that a tenant has is 'security of tenure'. This means that he can only be evicted from the property if the landlord follows the procedure laid down in the Act of Parliament which regulates that tenancy. In the 1980s, when the Rent Act 1977 applied to most tenancies, it was very difficult (and sometimes impossible) for landlords to evict tenants. Because of this, a landlord would sometimes try to claim that a letting was a licence so he could repossess his property through the courts. But in an important case in 1985, the courts ruled that whether an agreement is a tenancy or a licence depends upon the facts of the case and not what the agreement is called. For example, if the occupier has 'exclusive occupation' of all or part of the property and pays rent, then his occupation is normally deemed to be a tenancy, even if the document is called a 'licence agreement'. However, if the occupier receives services (such as board and cleaning) as in bed-and-breakfast accommodation, then the occupation will usually be a licence.

There is little incentive nowadays for landlords to try to get round the legislation, as they have much greater rights under the Housing Acts 1988 and 1996 which apply to most new tenancies today (for Scotland, the Housing (Scotland) Act 1988 applies). In particular, landlords can generally recover possession of their property through the courts, provided they follow the correct procedure. The legislation also implies various 'covenants' (i.e. legal obligations) into tenancies, the most important of which are the landlords' repairing covenants. These are considered further in the book, in particular in chapter 3.

Under the housing laws, tenancies will run on, after any initial fixed term has expired, until they are ended in a recognised way. The most common ways for a tenancy to end are by what lawyers called 'surrender', i.e. if the tenant vacates/gives up possession of the property, or by the court making an order for possession. This is discussed in more detail in chapters 7 and 8. Some landlords mistakenly think that a tenancy ends when the fixed term ends and that if tenants stay on after this, they are 'squatters'. This is not the case; they still have a valid tenancy.

It is perhaps also worth mentioning that someone occupying a property under a tenancy, whether it is an assured shorthold tenancy (AST) in England & Wales, a short assured tenancy (SAT) in Scotland or a Rent Act tenancy, cannot acquire 'squatters rights' over the property, however long they stay there. The only situation where this could conceivably happen is where the tenant stops paying rent and has no contact whatsoever with the landlord for a period of more than 12 years. This is not going to happen very often!

As mentioned above, when a landlord grants a tenancy of a property to a tenant, he loses many of his rights over the property in exchange for the right to receive rent. This means that he loses the right to deal with or enter the property and can only do so with the permission of the tenant. This is the case even if you want to enter the property for a legitimate purpose, such as the quarterly inspection or the annual gas check. If the tenant forbids you to enter, any attempt to do so will be trespass (even though by forbidding you access the tenant may be in breach of his tenancy agreement). This remains the case even if the tenant is in arrears of rent. Many landlords find this hard to understand or accept and feel that as they own the property they have the right to come and go as they wish. This is not the case; by granting a tenancy you lose control over the property and this passes to the tenant. You will only recover the right to deal directly with the property again once the tenant has vacated.

Set out below are some of the most important types of tenancy and licence agreement that exist. In this book I primarily concentrate on ASTs. However, I have included comments on assured tenancies (ATs), Rent Act tenancies and licences where appropriate.

Tenancies

Assured tenancy (AT)

Almost all tenancies that are granted nowadays are assured tenancies. The tenant has exclusive occupation of all or part of the property and the landlord has the right to charge a market rent. The landlord's rights (or 'grounds') to repossess the property are as laid down in the Housing Act 1988 (in Scotland, the Housing (Scotland) Act 1988), the most important being to recover possession as of right if the tenant falls into rent arrears of more than two months (in Scotland, rent arrears of more than three months).

Assured shorthold tenancy (AST)

Assured shorthold tenancies are a type or sub-group of assured tenancy, where the landlord has the additional right to recover property at the end of the fixed term, the 'shorthold' ground, provided the proper notices have been served on the tenant. ASTs are the most common type of tenancy granted today, as most tenancies are now automatically ASTs unless the landlord specifies otherwise. In this book, unless otherwise stated, it is assumed that the tenancy under discussion is an AST.

Short assured tenancy (SAT) in Scotland

This is similar to an AST, but the tenancy agreement must specify that it is a SAT and the correct notice must be served, otherwise it is an assured tenancy.

Rent Act tenancies

If a tenancy was granted before 15 January 1989 (2 January 1989 in Scotland), it will be regulated by the Rent Act 1977 (or the Rent Act (Scotland) 1984). This Act was more favourable to tenants; for example, it is more difficult for the landlord to evict tenants, and he can normally only charge a 'fair rent'. Tenancies under the Rent Act can be either 'protected' or 'statutory', but for the purposes of this book I will refer to them all as Rent Act tenancies. As Rent Act tenancies are by their nature a shrinking category, less consideration will be given to them in this book. Note that you cannot convert a Rent Act tenancy to an AST by simply giving the tenant a new fixed-term agreement with Assured Shorthold Tenancy written at the top; whatever the agreement document states, the tenancy will remain a Rent Act tenancy.

Agricultural tenancies

Agricultural tenancies are not covered in this book.

Company lets

If a property is let to a company as opposed to an individual, then much of the current legislation which protects tenants' rights (e.g. in the Housing Acts 1988 and 1996) will not apply. In the past this was sometimes used as a device to prevent the tenant getting security of tenure. However, this is now no longer necessary. It is generally assumed in this book that the tenant will be an individual and not a company.

Lettings at a very high or a very low rent

If the rent is more than £25,000 per annum (this upper limit does not apply in Scotland) or less than £250 per annum (£1,000 per annum in Greater London), or less than £6 per week in Scotland, the tenancy is specifically excluded from statutory protection as set out in the Housing Act 1988 and the tenancy will by default be regulated under the 'common law', in the same way that tenancies with resident landlords are, as discussed below.

Holiday lets

If a property is let for a bona fide holiday, normally for a period of weeks rather than months, the landlord can usually evict the occupiers if they refuse to leave, without getting a court order.

Licences

Lodgers

This is where someone lets a furnished room in his own home. The lodger has fewer rights (see below) and the landlord can evict him without getting a court order. Income up to a specified limit (currently £4,250) is normally exempt from tax.

Lettings which can be either a tenancy or a licence

Houses in multiple occupation (HMOs)

This is where a number of people occupy the same property but do not form a single 'household'. These can be tenancies; for example, where individuals rent their own room (and have separate tenancy agreements) but share other living accommodation (such as kitchen and bathroom) with other tenants, or licences; for example, where homeless people are housed in bed-and-breakfast accommodation in a hostel.

Local authorities have additional regulatory powers in respect of HMOs to ensure that they are of a proper standard of repair and that facilities are provided to a specified standard. The Housing Act 2004 provides for mandatory licensing by local authorities of some types of HMO, but at the time of writing this part of the Act has not yet come into force.

Do note that the Housing Act 2004 does not apply in Scotland. However, the Housing (Scotland) Bill is currently going through the Scottish

Parliament which provides for licensing by local authorities of some types of HMO. However, at the time of writing this Bill has not yet become law. For information with regard to the progress of the Bill, go to www.scottish. parliament.uk/business/bills/billsInProgress/housing.htm.

Employees

If an employee is required to occupy accommodation for the purposes of his employment, then this will be a licence and not a tenancy. Otherwise, the accommodation will normally be a tenancy, provided of course that the other elements of a tenancy, as discussed above, apply.

Other

There are always exceptions to the rules. If there is something unusual about your property or the terms upon which you intend to let it, you should seek independent legal advice.

Note

This book does not cover tenancies where part of the premises are used for a business, e.g. a manager's flat in licensed premises.

Resident landlords

Where the owner of the property lives in the same building, a letting is generally excluded from the definition of an AT (or AST). But the resident landlord rules cannot apply if the landlord is a company, and the landlord must be occupying the property as his main home at the time the tenancy is granted. There are two types of resident landlord situation that now apply:

1. Where the landlord shares accommodation with a licensee (i.e. lodgers).

2. Where the tenant occupies self-contained accommodation in the same building, provided this is not a purpose-built block of flats (e.g.

if the landlord has converted a large house into flats and lives in one of them). Here, a tenancy will be created but it will be regulated under the 'common law' and not the Housing Act 1988.

In Scotland, the situation is different: a tenant who occupies self-contained accommodation in a converted house would automatically be on an AT. To fall outside the Housing (Scotland) Act 1988, the landlord must have some means of access through the tenant's accommodation or vice versa.

Resident landlords have the following legal advantages:

- The tenant cannot refer the rent to the Rent Assessment Committee.
- The minimum two-month notice period as for shortholds does not apply.
- The protection from eviction legislation does not always apply (but see chapter 7).
- The statutory succession provisions do not apply (see below).

However:

- Resident landlords cannot use the accelerated possession procedure (see chapter 7) if they need to evict their tenants.

Note

If the landlord (or all of them if there is more than one) ceases to live at the property as his (or their) main home, the resident landlord exceptions will cease to apply.

New tenancies today

To summarise, as stated above, if a new tenancy is created, it will normally be an AST. This will happen automatically once the tenant gets into occupation, and a landlord cannot prevent a tenancy arising and avoid his legal obligations simply by failing to give a written agreement.

There are exceptions where an AST will not be created, and these are where there is a resident landlord or if the rent is very high or very low, or where the tenant is a limited company. A new AT will normally only be created nowadays when a long (e.g. 99-year) lease comes to an end or when a family member 'inherits' a Rent Act tenancy.

In Scotland, a new tenancy created will only be a SAT if the correct form of tenancy agreement is used and an AT5 notice (see below) is served on the tenant prior to him signing the tenancy agreement. If the tenancy agreement is not properly drawn up as a SAT, the AT5 notice is not served or indeed if there is no written tenancy agreement, the tenancy will normally be an AT. A landlord cannot prevent a tenancy arising and avoid his legal obligations by failing to give a written agreement. If, in fact, the landlord does fail to give a written agreement rather than provide the tenant with a SAT, the tenant will then be entitled to additional rights and the landlord's ability to terminate the tenancy will be more limited.

Other legal matters landlords need to know

Fixed-term and periodic tenancies

Normally a tenancy agreement states that the tenancy is for a specific period of time (e.g. six months). This is known as a 'fixed-term tenancy'. However, once the fixed term comes to an end, this does not mean that the tenant has to leave. The law will imply that the tenancy continues on the same terms as the fixed-term tenancy, but on a periodic basis; the period being based on how the rent is paid. This is called a 'periodic tenancy'.

So, if the rent is paid monthly, it will be a monthly periodic tenancy, if paid weekly, it will be a weekly periodic tenancy, and if paid quarterly, it will be a quarterly periodic tenancy. The first period will start the day after the fixed term ends. Say this is Monday 1 January. If the tenancy is a weekly periodic one, the next period will start on Monday 8 January, and if it is a monthly one, the next period will start on 1 February, and so on. On the whole, it is advisable that the period should be either weekly or monthly. Periodic tenancies can continue indefinitely, until the landlord or tenant does something to bring the tenancy to an end.

In Scotland, once the fixed term comes to an end the tenancy will continue on the same terms and conditions as the fixed-term tenancy for the same period as the original tenancy agreement. So, if the original tenancy agreement was for six months, the tenancy will continue for a further six months.

Note that a tenant cannot turn into a 'squatter' if he stays on after his tenancy agreement has come to an end.

Section 20 notices

Prior to 28 February 1997, it was necessary to serve a special notice (called a 'Section 20 notice', because it was required by Section 20 of the Housing Act 1988) on a tenant, before a tenancy was created, if you wanted that tenancy to be an AST. This caused many problems for inexperienced landlords, as the notice had to contain certain prescribed information and was invalid if it did not. Once a tenancy had started, it was impossible for it to be converted into an AST, if no Section 20 notice had been served or if the notice served was defective (although the courts have been prepared in some recent cases to overlook minor errors in Section 20 notices). Happily, Section 20 notices are no longer necessary for new tenancies as they were made redundant by the Housing Act 1996, which came into force (so far as Section 20 notices were concerned) on 28 February 1997. Section 20 notices are still important, however, for tenancies created between 15 January 1989 and 27 February 1997.

In Scotland, it is necessary to serve a notice called an AT5 on the tenant prior to entering into the tenancy agreement for it to be a SAT.

Guarantees

If a landlord is uncertain whether a tenant will be able to pay the rent, he can take security in the form of a guarantee. This is where someone else signs an agreement to confirm that he will pay the rent and any money due from the tenant, if the tenant defaults on his payments. For example, guarantees are normally taken from students' parents in student lets. If the student then leaves the property owing rent, the landlord can sue the guarantor for the student's rent arrears. A guarantee can either be included in the tenancy agreement itself, which the guarantor will sign as well as the tenants, or there can be a separate guarantee deed.

Note that if a new tenancy agreement is signed between the landlord and the tenant (particularly where there are changes; for example, if the rent has been increased), a new form of guarantee should also be signed with the guarantor, as the old guarantee deed may no longer be valid.

Joint and several liability

Where more than one tenant has signed a tenancy agreement, then the general rule is that they will all be 'jointly and severally' liable for the rent. For example, say four students (Matthew, Mark, Luke and John) are renting a house together and they all sign the same tenancy agreement for a total rent of £400 per month. They will no doubt have agreed between themselves that they will each pay £100 per month. However, if one of the four tenants, Mark, then stops paying his share (e.g. if he leaves the house), the landlord is entitled to claim the outstanding rent from any of the tenants, not just from Mark. The landlord is not bound by the tenants' own agreement to pay £100 each. So, if one of the tenants, say John, is wealthy, the landlord can sue just John and get a judgment against him for the outstanding rent, even though he has paid his share.

Also, if the landlord has taken a guarantee from the student's parents (as is often done in student lets), he can normally claim the whole of any outstanding rent from any one parent guarantor, as the parent will effectively be guaranteeing the whole of the rent, not just his son's share. This can be avoided by limiting the guarantor's liability, for example to a specified sum of money.

Letting your own home

If you have lived or are going to live in the property as your main residence, you have an additional mandatory ground for possession available: Ground 1 in Schedule 2 of the Housing Act 1988 (in Scotland, Ground 1 in Schedule 5 of the Housing (Scotland) Act 1988). To take advantage of this, you need to give the tenants notice that you may be recovering possession of the property under this ground (see chapter 5 for further information). But as most tenancy agreements nowadays are ASTs, there seems little point in using this ground, particularly as the accelerated possession procedure is no longer available for it.

Premiums

This is the term used where a sum of money is paid for a lease or tenancy. It is common practice with long leases. With short-term tenancies, they were specifically forbidden in the Rent Act 1977. They are not illegal now for ATs and ASTs under the Housing Act 1988. In Scotland, they are generally prohibited in terms of Section 27 of the Housing (Scotland) Act 1988.

However, even where permitted, they are generally inadvisable, as if they are charged, the tenancy will have to be signed as a deed, they may affect the stamp duty payable, and they will affect the landlord's right to prohibit assignment (see chapter 5).

Succession rights

Having a tenancy is a property right, like owning a house or a flat on a long lease. If a tenant dies, his tenancy does not always die with him. If a tenancy is a joint one (i.e. if more than one person has signed the tenancy agreement), then it will become the sole property of the remaining tenant. On the death of a sole tenant, provided the tenancy is one carrying succession rights, it will generally pass either to the spouse or, for Rent Act tenancies, provided certain conditions are met, to a member of the tenant's family (further information is given in chapter 8). It is beyond the scope of this book to go into the succession rules in any detail; if they are relevant to you, you should take legal advice.

Eviction of tenants and eviction notices

The eviction procedure and the various notices (Section 21 – notices requiring possession, and Section 8 – notices seeking possession) are discussed in chapter 8. In Scotland, the relevant notices are the Section 33 notice, the notice to quit and the AT6 notice.

The winds of change ...

Housing law is constantly changing and at the time of writing the most recent new act is the Housing Act 2004. Most of this Act has not yet come into effect, but it will be discussed where appropriate below. It incudes changes to the way environmental health authorities assess unfit properties, mandatory licensing for some HMO properties and a mandatory tenancy deposit scheme.

Further proposals to reform housing law in England & Wales are being considered by the Law Commission and a Bill may be introduced in 2005 or 2006. The proposals will bring about major changes, although the main features of ASTs (e.g. the right to charge a market rent and the shorthold ground for possession) will probably remain as they are. Although the changes are likely to be featured in the press, landlords should ensure that they are kept informed; for example, by joining a landlords' association or by subscribing to a suitable newsletter or journal, or via the author's online service. Details of these proposals can be found on the Law Commission's website, www.lawcom.gov.uk, and on the author's website, www.landlord law.co.uk (Law Reform section).

In Scotland, the Antisocial Behaviour, Etc. (Scotland) Act 2004 includes provision for the registration of landlords with the local authority. This means that it is unlawful for you to let out residential property as a landlord unless the local authority approves of you. There are also penalties against the landlord if his property is occupied by antisocial tenants. The part of the Act affecting landlords comes into force in November 2005. It affects all landlords and makes no distinction between short and long leases. As well as leases, it also applies to occupancy arrangements and accordingly it seems that owners who have, or wish to have, a lodger will have to register with their local authority as landlords. It is therefore recommended that anyone considering letting out their property or taking in a lodger, and indeed existing landlords, should contact their local authority to obtain details on registration.

CHAPTER 2

Initial considerations

A lot of careful thought is required before letting a property or acquiring a property to let. Different considerations will apply, depending on the type of property you wish to let and the reasons for letting. For example:

- **Your own home.** There are two main reasons why people let their own homes: (1) they are going abroad for a period of time and will require it on their return; and (2) they are unable to sell their property, for example due to negative equity. If you intend to live in the property again yourself, you will want to be particularly careful with your choice of tenant, especially if your own furniture is left in the property.

- **Your second home.** You may have a second home which you wish to rent out as a holiday home to earn an income for the periods when you do not wish to stay in it yourself. As you will not, in the nature of things, have your main home local to the property, it is probably best to consider using one of the specialist holiday country cottage letting agencies, at least, to start with.

- **Inheritance.** You may have inherited a property, perhaps on the death of your parents, and be considering letting it for an income, rather than selling it. You have slightly more flexibility here because if the property is unsuitable for letting, you can sell it and buy another more viable property with the proceeds of the sale.

- **Buy-to-let.** You may be considering purchasing an investment property specifically for letting. See the section below for further details on this.

'Location, location, location'

When letting a property its location is all-important. On this will depend the type of tenant you are likely to attract and the level of rent you will be able to achieve. For example, take two identical properties:

1. One is in a popular residential area in a county town, positioned halfway between the university and the centre. This property will be very easy to let and should achieve an above average rent (provided it is in good condition).

2. The other is in a run down part of a large 'inner-city' area, with high unemployment. This property will probably be very difficult to let unless you are prepared to take Housing Benefit tenants. Even then, particularly if the property is in an insalubrious part of town, you may find it impossible to let the property at all.

Even within a comparatively small area, conditions may change. A landlord of a property only a few miles from property 1 above, may find it harder to let or be unable to achieve such a good rent.

Also, conditions change over time. When letting student accommodation, for example, it is important that the property is available in June/July when most students are looking to take on a tenancy for the following academic year. Also, rents may increase in the short term if a company in the area is looking to relocate a large number of staff who are all looking for rented accommodation.

The location of a property will also, to a large extent, determine the type of tenancy you will have. For example:

- **'Good' areas.** These will be suitable for high-class assured shorthold tenancies (ASTs) (or short assured tenancies (SATs) in Scotland). These are usually the most trouble-free tenancies, as you can attract good quality tenants who will look after the property and pay promptly. Your initial investment, however, will be greater as the purchase price will probably be high and tenants will expect the property to be in good condition, with good quality fixtures and fittings.

- **Country properties.** Often the most suitable type of letting here will be holiday lets. These can be remunerative, particularly if the property is attractive and in beautiful countryside with local holiday attractions. Again, your investment may be high as holiday makers expect a high standard of comfort and facilities nowadays. Also, you may find that some items may need replacing frequently if holiday makers walk off with them.

- **Inner cities.** This is the type of area where you will find more HMOs and Housing Benefit tenants. These types of lettings are more time-consuming (particularly the HMOs) and you will probably have more problem tenants. However, with the right property and a careful choice of tenant, landlords can do well.

A landlord says ...

'If it is not good enough for you, it is probably not good enough for anyone else to live in.'

Other considerations

What is your intended type of tenant?

Different types of tenant will be attracted to different types of property. You should do some research into the market and decide what sector you will aim at, for example students, contract staff, Housing Benefit tenants. Some areas of the market are more profitable and some more labour-intensive. All will have different requirements which need to be borne in mind when purchasing a property and preparing it for letting.

Building or other work

The property as it stands may be unsuitable for letting, or for letting to the type of tenant you are seeking. For example, extensive alterations may be necessary if you intend the property to be an HMO. You should cost very carefully the building work necessary, and any ongoing costs, making sure that you have considered all the legal requirements that landlords are subject to, for example his responsibilities to keep the property in repair (see chapter 3). Bear in mind also that a property let to tenants will generally need more redecoration and other work than your own home. If there is likely to be a rapid turnaround of tenants, you may well find that you are having to redecorate at least part of the property before every new, or every alternate new, letting if you wish to attract good quality tenants. If the cost is going to render the project economically unviable, it is better to find this out now rather than after the work has been done.

Fixtures and fittings/furniture

Again, you need to consider the cost of fitting the property for letting, bearing in mind the product safety regulations discussed in chapter 3. Quality tenants will expect good quality fittings and 'white' goods (e.g. fridges, washing machines and cookers) in the property as standard, and will want furniture that is comfortable and attractive. Ensure that your budget is sufficient to provide for this.

A landlord says ...

'I always ask myself, 'Who is going to live in the property and if I were him, what would I want'?'

The availability of grants

Sometimes, local authority grants are available for improvement work on properties to be let. The availability of grants will vary from authority to authority and from time to time. You should speak to your local authority at the outset to see what is available. The type of grants that may be available include grants for property improvement/repairs, insulation, energy efficiency works, and for fire prevention works. Grants are normally awarded on an annual basis. If you are not successful one year, try again the next!

Remember that if you do get a grant, you may have to pay at least part of it back if you sell the property within five years.

A landlord says ...

'A ropey property in an area that the local authority wants smartening up will usually get a grant.'

Furnished or unfurnished?

For some types of letting you will have no choice; for example, students will not want unfurnished properties. Properties let unfurnished are more suitable for longer lets, for example to families who have their own furniture, and will generally achieve a lower rent. You will obtain a higher rent from furnished properties, especially if you are letting to professional people who require short-term accommodation because of work-related moves.

Achievable rent/financial considerations

Be realistic when considering rent. A property marketed at too high a rent is unlikely to find a tenant. When budgeting at this stage, it would be wise to allow for a slightly lower rent than you actually expect to achieve. Also, bear in mind that your actual earnings will be less than the monthly rent, even taking into account regular expenses such as mortgage payments. All rented properties will be empty for a period of time between tenants (known as 'voids'); also, you will have maintenance costs, agency fees (if you are letting via an agency) and probably other fees as well.

A landlord says ...

'I always budget on the basis that the property will only be let for ten months in the year.'

Tenant default

Always remember that even the best tenants can fall on hard times and can default on their rent. This may result in you having to evict them, which will mean legal expenses and a period without rent (as tenants rarely pay rent if they are being evicted). The likelihood of tenant default is far more likely in lower-quality HMOs, but it can occur in any type of property. Although tenant default is less likely in better quality lettings, when it does occur it will usually be more expensive – you are more likely to need a possession order and, of course, the rental you are losing is higher.

On the whole, most tenants are satisfactory. However, every landlord who lets for any period of time will have a bad tenant from time to time, and probably at least one tenant who will need evicting. Remember that 'Murphy's law' applies to residential letting as it does to every other area of life, and you will probably have your bad experience (if you have one) at the worst possible time. Try to guard against this and keep a special fund to pay for expenses should this type of thing happen.

Buy-to-let

Buy-to-let is popular and it is common to see advertisements for mortgages specifically for investment properties in the residential letting field. Many of these buy-to-let mortgage schemes are very good, and it is certainly worth considering using them to purchase a property for residential letting if you wish to invest but you do not have enough funds to buy outright. But the exercise should be carefully costed, particularly if the mortgage will be for a high percentage of the equity of the property.

When purchasing a property to let first you need to consider, 'What is my overall investment objective?' For example:

- You may be looking to purchase a house for your son while he is at university (a common arrangement is for the property to be let to the son and, say, three friends – the friends paying rent and the son living rent-free). This is a short-term objective, i.e. to provide accommodation for him for a limited period (normally three to four years) and then to sell the property, hopefully at a profit to reimburse you for the maintenance costs of supporting your son.

- Alternatively, you may be looking for an income to supplement a pension. This is a long-term objective.

What type of property should you purchase? There are three things to consider:

1. Your investment objective.

2. Whether you want rental income or capital growth as a priority. For example, if you have a good job, you may be looking for capital

investment, whereas if you are retired, you may want to live on the income.

3.   Can you visualise a situation where you will want to sell the property quickly? If the answer is yes, then you should look at properties in a prime location, as location sells. Do not look at good rental properties which will be difficult to sell.

You should note the following points:

- Do not buy in a poor location just to get in on the property market. What if you cannot let or sell it?

- Beware properties with structural faults. They may show a good rental return but may be impossible to sell. Leave these for the professional investor.

- Flats on long leases – these can be a good investment if you get the right one. However, there are many rogue landlords and poorly drafted leases, so be careful.

- Be very wary indeed of very cheap properties, particularly in poor and run-down areas. You may be taking on a liability rather than an investment.

- Buy new properties rather than old, preferably with small gardens – they will generally need less maintenance.

- Go for smaller properties (not more than two to three bedrooms); they will be easier to market and let than larger ones.

- Take proper advice, particularly if you are on a limited income.

Buying properties with existing tenants

If you are buying a property which is already tenanted, you should check very carefully the status of the existing tenancies. It may be wise to choose a solicitor who has some knowledge of residential lettings to do your conveyancing, rather than a cut-price firm where conveyancing is done on a 'conveyor belt' basis by unqualified staff. The following points are important:

- Establish the date when each tenancy **first** started.

- Make sure you obtain a copy of the initial tenancy agreement as well as the most recent one (if there has been more than one).

- If the tenancy began between 15 January 1989 and 28 February 1997, make sure that a Section 20 notice (explained in chapter 1) was served on the tenant and that you have a copy of the notice that was served and evidence that it was served prior to the tenancy being entered into (as otherwise you will not be able to evict the tenant under the shorthold ground). Ideally, you should have a statutory declaration from the person who served the notice on the tenant which exhibits a copy of the notice served. In Scotland, check to see if it is a short assured tenancy or an assured tenancy (AT).

- If the tenant first went into the property before 15 January 1989, then he will be a Rent Act tenant and you will find it very difficult, if not impossible, to evict him, should this become necessary. Also, you will not be able to charge more than the registered 'fair rent', which may be lower than the current market rent.

- Beware if there is no documentation regarding the tenancy.

Tip

If you are considering buying a property at auction, *Buying Bargains at Property Auctions* by Howard Gooddie (an extremely experienced auctioneer), also published by Lawpack, will be very helpful.

Houses in multiple occupation

The legal definition of a house in multiple occupation (HMO) has recently been changed by the Housing Act 2004 and the full definition is set out in Sections 254 to 263 of that Act and in Schedule 14. You can read the Act in full on the internet in the legislation section of www.hmso.gov.uk. It is a very long definition and it is not practical to reproduce it here.

However, basically an HMO is where people who are not related or living as a family unit live in the same property as their home and share at least some facilities or accommodation. This wording should not be regarded as a definition, however, and if you are uncertain whether the HMO regulations apply to your property, you will need to check the full definition or seek legal advice.

At the time of writing, this new legal definition has only just come into force and we will have to wait and see how it will be interpreted by the courts.

The Housing Act 2004 contains provisions regarding mandatory licensing by local authorities of certain HMOs (it is believed that this will be HMOs with more than five occupants and which have three or more storeys), plus the power to approve the licensing of other properties. However, these provisions have not yet come into force. Landlords should keep themselves informed regarding the implementation of this Act, for example by joining a landlords' association or via the author's website at www.landlordlaw.co.uk.

However, under earlier legislation, local authorities already have the power to require HMOs to be licensed in their area and there are mandatory licensing schemes in many areas. It is important, therefore, that new landlords, who think that their property may fall within the category of an HMO, speak to the Housing Officer at the environmental health department of their local authority and seek advice regarding their legal obligations. These are the best people to seek advice from as it is they who will be enforcing the legislation, and they will generally be more aware of recent developments than solicitors or other legal advisers.

The Housing Act 2004 does not apply in Scotland, but the Housing (Scotland) Bill is currently making its way through Parliament. Part 4 of the Bill deals with licensing of HMOs. In terms of Section 118 of that Bill, an HMO is defined as 'any living accommodation occupied by three or more persons who are not all members of the same family, or of one or other of two families'. This Housing Bill has not been passed by the Scottish Parliament and there may be some amendment to the provisions by the time it becomes law. At present, the best advice is to check with your local authority with regard to their current licensing and other requirements with regard to HMOs.

HMOs need a lot of management and are probably best managed by the landlord rather than a letting agent. Landlords should ideally visit their properties at least once a week. A week is a long time in an HMO, particularly where there are many tenants. One bad tenant can affect the whole household, and the landlord has a duty of care to his other tenants. A landlord of an HMO needs to know what is going on in his property.

An HMO is subject to more regulations than a normal tenancy. These regulations are largely concerned about the risk involved where people who do not know each other live in close proximity. Also, HMO tenants tend to be more transitory and there is often a more rapid turnover. People do not usually stay in an HMO on a long-term basis by choice. There are different categories of HMO and a local authority will specify standards that need to be adhered to for each category, such as the space needed for each occupier and the size of rooms allowable, heating, ventilation, facilities, fire precautions, and management standards.

In addition to the normal landlord's obligations (discussed in chapter 3), the landlord of an HMO must also do the following:

- Maintain the water supply and drainage, and the facilities for heating and hot water are in good working order.

- Not interrupt the supply of water, gas, or electricity unreasonably.

- Keep shared facilities (such as baths, sanitary conveniences, sinks, fridges, cookers) clean and in proper working order.

- Make sure that the living accommodation is in a clean condition at the start of each resident's occupation.

- Keep windows and ventilation facilities in good repair and proper working order.

- Take precautions to ensure that the premises are safe.

- Keep all fire escapes and fire precautions in good repair and free from obstruction.

- Keep the common parts of the property (e.g. staircases, passageways, landings and balconies) clean, in a good state of repair, and free from obstruction, so as not to block a means of escape in the case of fire or any other emergency.

- Maintain any outbuildings and yards that form part of the HMO.

- Provide adequate rubbish bins and ensure that rubbish is removed regularly.

- Ensure a notice is displayed giving the name, address, and telephone number of the manager of the HMO.

- Where there is a local registration scheme, provide the local authority with details of occupiers and any changes in occupancy.

Further details of the landlord's responsibilities are set out in the 'Housing (Management of Houses in Multiple Occupation) Regulations 1990', available from The Stationery Office, or online at www.legislation.hmso.gov.uk (Statutory Instrument 1990 Number 830).

The HMO regulations are largely policed by the environmental health departments of local authorities. They have extensive powers and, if necessary, they can take over the management of an HMO or, ultimately, issue a compulsory purchase order. However, these draconian powers are not usually used except as a final resort.

Local authorities are sometimes proactive and will inspect HMOs of their own volition. However, more usually they are reactive and will only inspect it if an HMO has been drawn to their attention. This can be by neighbours worried about noise and rubbish, other tenants concerned about antisocial behaviour, concerned parents of students, or indeed the tenants themselves complaining about the condition of the property. Once a complaint has been received, they have a duty to investigate.

However, although the local authority powers are very large, they normally prefer to help landlords put problems right rather than prosecute. Prosecution will normally only be used as a last resort. If landlords follow their advice, they should not have a problem.

Tip

Before converting a house to an HMO, a landlord should consult with the environmental health department of his local authority to check that the property is suitable for conversion. A difference of a few inches in a room size can be crucial.

Local authority assistance

Because of the pressure on local authorities to rehouse the homeless and the reduction of their housing stock due to the right to buy, local authorities are becoming more reliant on the private sector to fulfil their statutory obligations. They are, therefore, often keen to assist landlords to bring more properties into use. Many local authorities have a special section looking at bringing empty homes back into use and there are often grants available to bring the property up to the required standard. For example, flats above shops are often targeted, although if they have not been used for residential purposes before, they may require planning permission for the change of use. Often local authorities will agree to enter into a leasing agreement with a landlord, whereby the landlord is paid rent by the local authority who will then be able to use the property to house homeless families. This is often attractive to landlords, as the rent is guaranteed by the local authority and they will also maintain the property. Even if the local authority is not able to enter into a leasing agreement, they will be able to assist in finding tenants and will often have a damage deposit guarantee scheme, to help prospective tenants who cannot afford to pay. New landlords, and experienced landlords seeking to purchase property in a new area, are therefore advised to contact their local authority to see what is available.

Many local authorities are keen to work with local landlords and will have a landlords' forum which landlords may find useful to join. Local authorities may also run an accreditation scheme that landlords can also join (see more on this in chapter 3).

Often the local authority website can provide information about their services, or visit the Local Authority Directory on the author's website at www.landlordlaw.co.uk.

Landlords' associations

If you are considering letting property, check to see if there is a landlords' association in your area. It may be prepared to give you some initial advice. If you decide to take the plunge and become a landlord, your landlords' association will be invaluable. You will normally, however, have to agree to comply with the association's code of practice as a condition of membership. Benefits of membership generally include:

- Regular meetings where you can hear speakers on subjects of interest to landlords and have an opportunity to speak to other, perhaps more experienced, landlords.

- Information on the latest housing legislation, rules and good practice.

- Practical advice and information.

- A list of approved suppliers, many of whom will offer discounts to members.

- Competitive property and contents insurance cover for members.

- A regular newsletter.

- The respect which usually flows from being a member of a recognised professional body.

Your local landlords' association may also operate a tenancy deposit scheme – see chapter 5.

Most landlords' associations are themselves members of the National Federation of Residential Landlords, which negotiates on behalf of private residential landlords with the government and with government departments. By being a member of your local association, you may be able to help influence government decisions affecting the private landlord.

Tip

To find the landlords' association for your area, call the National Federation of Residential Landlords (see the Appendix) or visit its website at www.nfrl.org.uk.

CHAPTER 3

Preparation of the property

Before preparing your property for letting, you should first ensure that you are legally entitled to let it to tenants.

Permission for letting

This may be necessary, for example:

- If the property is leasehold, you will need to check your lease carefully. Usually in a long lease you will need your own landlord's permission before subletting, or you may have to give notice. You should ensure that any terms in your lease are complied with.

- If there is a mortgage on the property, you will need to obtain the lender's permission to let. This is normally granted, although some lenders will only give consent subject to a small increase in the interest rate on the loan. If you do not obtain the lender's consent, strictly speaking you will be in breach of the mortgage agreement and he may be entitled to call in the loan. Any conditions imposed by the lender should be complied with.

Planning permission

This is not normally necessary unless you are 'developing' a property (e.g. converting a single home to a house in multiple occupation (HMO).

However, even if you are going to let the property as one unit, if you intend having more than six tenants, you should always check to see if planning permission is needed, as this may constitute a material change of use. Your local Planning Officer will advise you.

If planning permission is needed (e.g. if you are converting a property into a number of flats), the Planning Officer will probably be looking at the availability of parking, so do ensure that there is adequate parking at the property. He will also be considering such things as fire prevention, sound proofing, and compliance with the HMO regulations. If you are developing an HMO, it is important that you comply with all the requirements, as the environmental health department will inevitably find out about the property sooner or later (e.g. from the Benefit Office when your tenants claim benefit). If you do not have planning permission, they will then be serving enforcement notices on you. When planning permission is granted, it is important that you do not exceed the permitted number of tenants.

Remember that if you are carrying out any building works, you will also need to comply with building regulations. You should not confuse building regulations with planning permission; the two are separate and both must be complied with.

Tip

Watch out for agricultural restrictions on properties on farms; their use may be limited to occupation by farm workers.

Renovations and repairs

Once you have dealt with any preliminary legal requirements, you then need to put the property into a proper condition to let.

It is most important that the property is in a good condition before it is let. For example:

- Cutting costs and not having the property in a good state of repair will not attract good tenants which may result in problems later in the tenancy. Most people are not prepared to put up with poor quality accommodation nowadays.

- You may not have access during the letting.

- If the property is in poor repair, you will be vulnerable to claims by the tenants (who may be eligible for Legal Aid) who can apply for an injunction (or interdict in Scotland) and/or damages, or you may have a repairs notice served on you by the local authority.

- It is easier to ensure that the property is left in a good condition after the tenants leave, if it is in a good condition when they arrive.

- You will have complied with your legal obligations which will make it difficult for tenants to justify any non-compliance with their obligations (such as payment of rent).

A landlord has a duty to put a property into proper repair before it is let to tenants and to keep it in proper repair once it is let. Under the Landlord and Tenant Act 1985 (and the Housing (Scotland) Act 1987), private residential landlords are responsible for:

- the structure and exterior of the dwelling;

- installations for the supply of water, gas and electricity and for sanitation;

- basins, sinks, baths and other sanitary installations;

- heating and hot water installations.

If a tenancy forms part of a larger building which the landlord owns or has control over, then he is also responsible for keeping in repair the structure and exterior, and for keeping in repair and proper working order any installations located in any part of the building and which directly or indirectly serve the installations in the tenanted property. For example, in a block of flats the landlord will have to keep the common parts in repair, and also the other flats, but only if any disrepair interferes with his tenants' use of their flat and the common parts they are entitled to use.

If you are considering converting a property to an HMO, there will be other standards you will have to comply with and you should consult your local authority before doing any work (see HMO section above).

For major works, you may wish to consider employing a qualified architect or surveyor to oversee it. As discussed above, you may be eligible for a local authority grant for works, particularly if you are converting a property to an HMO. You will usually need two written estimates of the cost. As always with building works, you need to be careful with your choice of builder. You may wish to consider using one who belongs to a trade association which operates a guarantee scheme, such as those run by the Building Employees Confederation or the Federation of Master Builders.

Remember that if a property is in poor condition, the local authority environmental health department may serve a repairs notice on you, and has draconian powers to enforce this if necessary.

A landlord says ...

'You need to get a property right from the outset – it is very difficult to get routine improvements done if tenants are in occupation.'

Building regulations

Before carrying out any building work, you need to check whether building regulations apply. If they do, you will have to obtain approval of your proposed works before they start and they will have to be inspected after completion. Your architect/surveyor/builder should be able to arrange this for you.

Heating

It will be difficult to let the property unless it has proper heating, and this generally means central heating. Providing proper heating will also mean that tenants are less likely to use their own heating devices, such as gas cylinder heaters, which may be dangerous. It is often a good idea to specify in the tenancy agreement that the heating facilities provided (e.g. central heating) must be used and to prohibit other forms of heating, particularly oil and gas cylinder heaters.

Condensation

This is mentioned here as it is probably the most common complaint about properties nationwide. It can be avoided by landlords installing proper heating, insulation and ventilation. However, it is sometimes caused by tenants not heating the property and not opening the windows. If this is likely to be a problem, it might be a good idea for the tenancy agreement to provide that the property should be heated to a certain specified level in the winter.

Gas regulations

The Gas Safety (Installation and Use) Regulations 1998

These are to ensure the safety of all gas appliances in all let properties and must be strictly adhered to. Badly maintained gas appliances can kill.

- All gas appliances (including mobile gas heaters) must be properly installed by a CORGI-registered plumber (see the Appendix for details).

- Before a property is let, and annually thereafter, all gas appliances must be checked by a CORGI-registered plumber.

- A copy of the gas certificate stating that a check has been done and detailing any work done must be handed to a tenant at the start of a tenancy and provided to him annually thereafter (within 28 days of the annual check being completed).

- For properties, such as holiday lets, where occupancy is under 28 days, a copy of the safety check record should be posted in a prominent position in the premises.

- A landlord cannot delegate maintenance or safety checks to a tenant.

- All gas certificates must be kept for at least two years, but landlords are advised to keep them for at least six years, just in case they are needed as evidence in any claim brought in respect of the property.

Remember, the landlord is ultimately responsible for the safety of all gas appliances in properties let by him. This means that if a tenant dies of carbon monoxide poisoning, the landlord is the one who will be prosecuted for manslaughter. The only way you can protect against this happening to you is to ensure that comprehensive checks are carried out each year by a CORGI-registered plumber, who is authorised to do the work, and to ensure that all complaints received from the tenant are dealt with immediately. Keep proper records of everything so you can prove, if necessary, that you have complied with the law.

The regulations are administered by the Health & Safety Executive, which is also the enforcing body. Breach of the regulations is a criminal offence punishable either by a fine of up to £5,000 for each offence, or an unlimited fine/imprisonment if the case is referred to the Crown Court.

Tip

Landlords should obtain the Health & Safety Executive Code of Practice and Guidance, which sets out the regulations and advises how they can best be complied with. The obligations of landlords are summarised in a leaflet called *A Guide to Landlords' Duties*, available free from HSE Books (see the Appendix).

Problems to watch out for:

- Dust and detritus in a gas appliance which can cause it to become unsafe. A sign of this is when the colour of the flame changes to a smoky yellow.

- Black soot deposits around gas appliances.

- Cracks in the cement blocks found in older fires and mobile heaters.

- Poor ventilation, caused by either a blocked flue or ventilation in a room (e.g. air bricks) becoming blocked, which can cause a build-up of carbon monoxide in the air.

- Gas leaks (e.g. if gas pipes become damaged). It is important to ensure that vulnerable pipes are protected.

Tip

For further advice about gas safety issues, landlords can ring the HSE Gas Safety Advice Line on 0800 300 363.

Electricity

At the time of writing, there are no specific regulations requiring certification for electrical wiring/installations in rented property. However, the landlord has a general duty to provide a safe environment and is strongly advised to have the electrical installations regularly checked. Remember that a common cause of fire is faulty electrical installations and the landlord can be found liable to the tenant for any losses. You will generally be protected from claims by tenants if you have the property inspected before the tenants go in, and deal with all complaints promptly.

If you intend to let to students, a students' union will generally require all properties on their list to have an annual inspection report covering the electrical installation at the property from an electrical contractor who is a member of the National Inspection Council for Electrical Installation Contractors (NICEIC). Further information can be obtained from your local college students' union.

A landlord says ...

'I was glad I had arranged for an electrical inspection when the Inspector found a live wire in one of the walls, due to unauthorised wall lights having been installed and then removed by the previous tenants.'

Fire safety

This is particularly important for HMOs, where there are strict regulations. However, it is important that this is considered for all properties, if only to protect your investment.

You should consider the following points when preparing a property for letting:

- All landlords are required by law to ensure that there is an adequate means of escape in case of fire.

- Try to protect the staircase, so that everyone can get out in an emergency, by fitting self-closing doors to all rooms.

- Fit smoke detectors to give warning in the event of a fire. For HMOs, these need to be interlinked mains-powered smoke detectors. For large HMOs, the smoke alarms need to be linked to a commercial fire alarm system.

- It should be possible for the front door to be opened at all times from the inside. Cylinder locks are better here than mortice locks which need to be unlocked with a key. If you feel a mortice lock is essential, get one with a thumb turn from the inside. Also possible but less satisfactory (because it can get lost or be stolen) is to have a spare key hanging by the door.

- Give new tenants an information pack regarding fire safety in the property.

- Place notices in HMOs showing exit routes in the case of fire, and the location of the nearest phone for calling the fire brigade.

- Consider having a fire blanket and a small dry powder extinguisher in the kitchen (but if the property is an HMO, discuss this with the Fire Officer).

- Try to make escape routes (e.g. passages and corridors) 'fire sterile', i.e. do not have anything that can burn on the walls – use emulsion paint rather than wallpaper or hessian covering.

For larger HMOs, you should also consider:

- Emergency lighting (this may be mandatory for some local authorities).

- Arranging means of escape through adjacent buildings.

- Fire-retardant curtains.

Make sure that you take proper advice on fire safety and get the necessary work done before the tenants move in. You should speak first to your local Environmental Health Officer; however, the fire safety department at your local fire brigade will often be pleased to advise.

Water

When converting properties into flats, the water company may have the right to install water meters. There may be problems thereafter with apportionment and payment of water bills if, for example, two or more flats have a shared water heater. Ideally, each flat should have its own water meter. Often, for example in HMOs, the landlord pays the water bills; however, if the water is metered, this may mean large bills for you, as tenants rarely economise on something that is free to them. If they are annoyed with you for any reason, they may even leave taps running deliberately.

An HMO landlord says ...

'If utility bills are in the name of tenants, they will often do a runner when the bills come in. I am not responsible for the bills, but I have all the bother of having to find another tenant.'

Fitting out the property

To a certain extent, the standard of fittings and furnishings will depend upon the type of tenant you are catering for. However, generally standards have increased recently and you will find it difficult to find good tenants if the property does not have good quality fittings and furniture. Obviously they should all comply with the product safety regulations described below.

Most people will now require as standard good quality 'white goods' (e.g. cookers, fridges, washing machines, etc.). Furniture should be attractive but hard wearing. Even if you are letting a property unfurnished, it will need to be carpeted and have curtains.

A landlord says ...

'It is best to use good quality carpeting as cheap carpets stain easily and are often difficult to clean.'

Product safety regulations

These regulations generally apply when a landlord is letting a property as a commercial venture. This includes properties which are being let via an agent. As a matter of good practice, however, the regulations should be complied with in all cases. If a landlord is letting his own home, say while he is working abroad for a year leaving his own furniture in the property, then the regulations will probably not apply.

The various product safety regulations apply to anything supplied as part of a property, but not permanently fixed.

A Trading Standards Officer says ...

'If in doubt, chuck it out.'

Furniture and furnishings

The Furniture and Furnishings (Fire) (Safety) Regulations apply to all furniture and soft furnishings which must be fire-safety compliant. Items covered include padded headboards, sofas, mattresses, pillows, cushions, nursery furniture, and cloth covers on seats. Make sure that all items carry the proper label.

Items which are exempt are furniture made before 1950 (and reupholstery of furniture made before that date), curtains and carpets, duvets, and sheets.

There is a very helpful guide to the regulations published by the Department of Trade and Industry, which can be obtained from your local Trading Standards Office, which will also be able to give you general advice.

Electrical equipment

The Electrical Equipment (Safety) Regulations control the supply of electrical equipment. This covers all electrical goods, i.e. kettles, TVs, fires, fridges, etc., which must be safe. It is best to have them tested by a bona fide qualified electrician, preferably annually. Keep records of all inspections and testing, with lists of the items inspected and details of their condition. Things to watch out for include:

- Plugs, which need to be sleeved.

- Old cookers, as the plates may become live if the insulation is old.

- Bare or damaged wire on leads.

- Small moveable objects which are more likely to be damaged through wear and tear.

Electrical items also need to comply with the Plugs and Sockets Safety Regulations; if they were purchased new recently, this should not be a problem.

Tip

These regulations do not apply to the tenant's own furniture and possessions. However, these must be removed when they leave the property.

The General Product Safety Regulations

The General Product Safety Regulations control the supply of general consumer products. These regulations cover general problems in properties, such as missing rungs in ladders, stepladders with faulty locking devices, and slippery carpets. Anything supplied in the property needs to be safe.

You need to ensure this, not only because you might become liable for prosecution under the regulations, but also because you might otherwise become liable for a civil claim for damages, if someone is injured as a result of the unsafe item. You should therefore always ensure that there are no unsafe items when properties are let, and make sure that repairs are done quickly, once they are brought to your attention by your tenant.

... and finally

The best way to deal with all these regulations is to draw up a full inventory of all upholstered furniture, electrical equipment, and general consumer products in the property, and make a note of their general condition. You should then make sure that all of any identified problems are dealt with before the property is let. This should also be done every time the property is vacated before reletting. Keep records of all checks (e.g. electrical checks) done, repairs and items replaced. Keep all invoices and receipts (you should also keep these to claim against tax).

The Trading Standards Office is the prosecuting authority for offences under these regulations. However, it will normally want to work with a landlord to put things right and will only prosecute as a last resort. It is always happy to advise and new landlords should contact their local office at an early stage as it usually has useful advice/fact sheets which landlords will find helpful.

A letting agent says ...

'In our experience, the better the condition of the property at the start of the tenancy, the less likelihood there is that the property will be left in a poor condition at the end of the tenancy.'

Insurance

You need to be sure that your insurance is suitable for rented property. If you are letting your own home, do not rely on your ordinary household insurance. In particular, ensure that your insurer knows that the property is rented. With insurance, you have a duty of good faith to tell the insurer all relevant factors. If you do not, the insurer can refuse to pay when a claim is made.

Even if you are only letting rooms in your own home, you need to check that you are adequately insured.

Insurance for rented properties generally needs to cover the following:

- The structure of the property.
- Landlord's contents, fittings and fixtures (the tenant generally insures his own possessions).

- Public liability – this is to cover you in the event of tenants or members of the general public making a claim in respect of personal injury or death, or damage to their possessions. Insurers recommend that this should be for a minimum of at least five million pounds. This sounds a lot, but claims from several people, particularly if they are seriously injured, could be extremely expensive.

- Loss of rent following damage to the property.

You might also wish to consider insurance cover for:

- The cost of finding alternative accommodation for your tenants.

- Legal expenses.

- Non-payment of rent (a rent guarantee policy).

If you take out any of these policies, it is wise to read the small print, which will usually specify actions that need to be taken before a claim can be made. For example, letters demanding payment of unpaid rent will normally need to be sent to the tenant within a specified period of time. If this is not done, cover may be refused.

If you are considering letting to asylum seekers, Housing Benefit tenants or students, be sure to check that the policy does not exclude these. Remember that tenants' circumstances can change; for example, they may go on benefit without you knowing about it. However, this would not stop your insurers refusing to pay when a claim is made.

As with all insurance, you also need to insure for the correct sum. If the structure of the property is underinsured, this will affect payouts not only when there is total destruction of the property but also for smaller claims, as insurers will say that you have only insured a proportion of the property. Your surveyor will be able to advise you of the current rebuilding costs.

Most landlords' associations will have a special insurance policy available for members and this is usually excellent value. If this is not available, you should consult an independent insurance broker for advice before taking out insurance.

There are now several insurance companies offering specialist policies for private residential landlords.

Note that if your tenancy agreement seeks to make the tenant liable should he breach the terms of your insurance policy (e.g. if he causes the premiums to increase) then you will need to provide a copy of the insurance policy, or an extract of the relevant parts, to the tenant. If you do not, the clause in the tenancy agreement may be invalid.

Rent

If you are a new landlord, it may be best to take professional advice when setting rent levels for the first time. Multiple occupancy (e.g. renting individual rooms in a property, to students say, on separate agreements) will often achieve a higher rent than letting the property as a whole, certainly if you are letting to tenants on Housing Benefit this will normally be the case. But this may then mean the property is classed as an HMO making the landlord liable under the more onerous HMO regulations. Also, if the landlord lets to a group of tenants on an agreement, he has the protection of joint and several liability (see chapter 1). Sources of information for local rental levels include: properties let by other agents, local papers and the internet (e.g. landlords' association websites).

The rental market is different from the selling market. Rental levels can fluctuate from one month to the next and from one area to another.

If you are including Council Tax and any utilities in the rent (as will often be the case with HMOs), you should, particularly if the property is being let to tenants on Housing Benefit, apportion the rent between pure rental and payment for each individual service or tax. Your tenancy agreement should make provision for the rent to increase in line with services or Council Tax.

A letting agent says ...

'We have a saying, 'The greedy man goes hungry'. Do not market at too high a price. Consider the difference between your losses with an empty property at a silly asking rent and your profits with a property let at a moderate rent. Remember, if the property is standing empty, you will still have outgoings to pay.'

Accreditation

Some local authorities, landlords' associations and student bodies are running accreditation schemes for landlords. Landlords who are members have to ensure that their properties meet the prescribed standards and comply with any other requirements of the scheme (such as bonding for damage deposits). They can then advertise their properties as accredited and take advantage of any local promotion of the scheme, for example through universities for student accommodation. Another advantage of membership is that training is also sometimes available for landlords as part of the scheme. Many schemes, particularly those run by local authorities, will include a landlords' forum where landlords can make their views known to the local authority and 'network' with other landlords. Further information and details of accreditation schemes near you can be obtained from the Accreditation Network, which has a website at www.anuk.org.uk.

CHAPTER 4

Finding a tenant

Letting agents

Using a letting agent is often a good idea. Sometimes it is essential; for example, if the landlord is not local to the property. It is essential that there is someone local to the property whom the tenant can contact if there is a problem, and who can keep an eye on it and inspect it regularly. Even if the landlord does live locally, he may not have sufficient time to manage the property properly, in which case again it is best to use an agent. However, if the landlord can manage the property himself, the financial returns will be higher, as he will not have to pay the agent's commission. Houses in multiple occupation (HMOs) are best managed by the landlord personally as letting agents are rarely able to give the degree of supervision that an HMO property requires.

Agents will charge a fee and this will usually be by way of a commission. They normally offer two types of service. One of these will be an introduction service where they find a tenant and the landlord manages the property thereafter. Their commission here will usually be in the region of one month's rent. Normally, however, they will prefer landlords to use their full management service. Here, their fees will be in the region of ten to 15 per cent of rents collected. Usually agents will also charge extra for providing an inventory, tenancy agreements, overseas telephone calls and other special services. The cheapest agent is not necessarily the best – the fact that they are cheap may mean that they are unqualified, give staff no training, and don't pay professional association subscription fees.

When choosing an agent, be aware that there are no statutory or other requirements for becoming a letting agent and that anyone can set up shop if they wish. It is important, therefore, to be extremely careful in your choice as there are a number of 'cowboy' firms around who provide a poor service. Remember that they will be looking after your valuable investment and a poor firm can cost you a lot of money. It is best to choose one which is a member of the National Approved Letting Scheme. This includes members of the Association of Residential Letting Agents (ARLA), the Royal Institute of Chartered Surveyors (RICS), and the National Association of Estate Agents (NAEA). If you use a member of one of these organisations, you can generally expect a higher standard of professional competence, a knowledge of the regulations, and fidelity bonding (a client money protection scheme).

However, there is still a great deal of variation between one firm and another, even among members of the National Approved Letting Scheme, and indeed between different offices of the same firm. Perhaps the most important thing is the calibre of the staff, their knowledge, training and general efficiency. When looking for an agent, ask around among friends and acquaintances, join a landlords' association and speak to other landlords about local agents at their meetings; speak to other landlords who have property with an agent you are thinking of using. All other things being equal, it is wise to choose an agent who has been in the area a long time. They will usually have a greater depth of knowledge, and local knowledge is very important in this field.

A careful choice of agent is very important, particularly if you are going to be living abroad, as it is not unknown for agents to go out of business, which normally means that the landlord loses rent paid to the agent but not yet paid to him, and the deposit (if there is no client's money protection scheme). This can put the landlord in financial difficulties if, for example, there are payments, such as mortgage payments, which need to be paid on the property, and he will be responsible for returning the deposit to the tenant. Also, the landlord will have to take over the management of the tenancy at what might be an extremely inconvenient moment.

A letting agent will almost invariably ask you to sign a management contract. Read this carefully. Make sure that it specifies that the agent will be responsible for carrying out the maintenance and safety check duties (e.g. regarding the Gas Regulations), and for keeping all associated records. The agent will also need authorisation to spend up to a specified sum on general repairs and maintenance. Check also that you are happy about all the clauses in the agreement, particularly those about termination of the agency agreement (sometimes a long notice period is specified) and about additional charges. If there is anything you do not understand, seek advice before signing.

Letting agents can deal with the preliminary aspects of evicting tenants (should this be necessary), such as writing letters and serving notices; but a solicitor will have to be instructed for any court proceedings. The agent can deal with this on your behalf if you wish, but the solicitor will need to see either a written authority from you confirming that the agent can give instructions on your behalf, or a power of attorney. Sometimes agents will offer to deal with legal proceedings on behalf of a landlord. This is not a good idea. The only people who can legally sign the court papers are the litigant himself or his solicitor. An agent is not authorised to sign on a landlord's behalf, even if he has power of attorney. Note also that if the landlord is out of the country, it is essential that a solicitor in England, Wales or Scotland is instructed, as the court will refuse to make an order unless there is an address for service in this country.

Note

I am informed by a District Judge that a common reason for rejecting claims for possession proceedings is that the court papers have been signed by the letting agent!

If you are going to be resident abroad, it is usually a good idea, in any case, to arrange for someone to have a power of attorney (either the letting agent, your solicitor, or a relative or trusted friend) so that if a problem arises while you are unavailable, someone is empowered to deal with it. However, unless you have absolute faith in that person, it is a good idea for the power of attorney to be limited (e.g. so he cannot sell the property and disappear with the proceeds!). A solicitor will be able to advise you and draft the power of attorney for you, or consult Lawpack's *Wills, Power of Attorney & Probate Guide.*

It is often a good idea for a new landlord to use a reputable agent to provide initial advice and to find the tenant, even if he wants to manage the property himself. An agent will be able to market the property at a suitable price and will have better contacts for finding a good tenant. Also, a good letting agent can often advise on small improvements to a property that can sometimes make all the difference in getting a tenant. Most letting agents nowadays will also have their own website where the property can be marketed.

> **Note**
>
> Corporate tenants (i.e. large companies looking for properties for their staff) will normally only rent via a reputable professional agent (normally only those who are members of ARLA or RICS). As these are usually excellent tenants, this is another good reason for using an agent.

Advertising for tenants

The following are some of the most common methods:

- **Newspapers and magazines.** You should choose the paper most likely to be read by your target class of tenant. Usually this will be the local paper. Most local papers will have a particular day in the week when local property is advertised, and may have a property supplement. However, sometimes a different paper may be appropriate. For example, holiday cottages are often advertised in the Sunday papers or in glossy magazines. If your tenants generally come from a particular large company in your area, they may have an in-house journal where you can advertise.

- **Shop windows.** This can be a cheap way of advertising a property if you are looking for a local tenant. Most newsagent shops offer this service.

- **Notice boards.** Perhaps the best example of this is university notice boards, if you wish to advertise properties for students. Be warned, however, that many student unions will only allow landlords who meet certain (often stringent) quality standards to advertise. Local businesses may, if you provide accommodation regularly for their staff, allow you to put a card on their notice board.

- **The internet.** This is now an important method of advertising properties. It is a particularly good way of advertising properties to students, as they almost always have free internet access via their university library. There is a number of online services nowadays which will advertise properties to rent for no charge. Landlords' associations often have a website where members can advertise their properties, or if you are a large landlord, you could consider setting up your own website. As time goes by, this will probably become one of the most important methods of advertising properties, both to rent and to sell.

The Property Misdescriptions Act 1991

It is not often realised that this Act can apply to advertising rented properties. This is when properties are being let by letting agents and by anyone carrying on a 'property development business'. This includes anyone who refurbishes a building with a view to letting it for profit. The Act provides that criminal sanctions are available against those who make untrue statements about properties.

It is therefore important that all statements you make about the property are true, both in your advertising and when you discuss the property with prospective tenants. As well as the criminal sanctions under the Act, if untruthful statements are made, the tenant may be entitled to cancel the tenancy agreement and claim back any money paid, under a legal rule known as 'misrepresentation'.

The paramount importance of a good tenant

Finding a good tenant is the single most important thing in letting a property (and good tenants can be worth a lot of money). If you have a good tenant, then any problems can be dealt with comparatively easily as the tenant will be reasonable about them (provided of course that you are, too). If you have a bad tenant, you will have nothing but trouble and may even end up out of pocket.

An example

A landlord lets to a 'hippy'-type family as he is anxious to have tenants in his empty property and the family say that they are desperate for accommodation. He is not entirely happy about them but feels that letting them in will be better than leaving the property empty. Once in, they proceed to redecorate the property, painting the walls black and all the radiators dark mauve. Numerous complaints are received from neighbours about their behaviour and loud music at night. There are several incidents when the police are called out and it is suspected that they are taking drugs. They pay one month's rent in advance but fail to pay any rent thereafter, and the landlord has to issue proceedings for possession to evict them. This process takes four months, by which time the rent arrears have risen to several thousand pounds. The night before the bailiff is due to come to evict them, they have a party, during the course of which several windows are broken, and other damage is done to the property. It is left in a filthy state with rubbish in all of the rooms. Much of the furniture has been either broken or stolen. The landlord is left with a property which needs several thousand pounds of work (including redecoration throughout and replacement of almost all the furniture) to make it fit for reletting, a bill from his solicitors for the eviction proceedings, and no chance of recovery from the tenants who have disappeared without trace.

This scenario is fictitious but all of the individual elements are drawn from the writer's own experience as a solicitor involved in evicting tenants. An experience as dire as this is rare; however, this does not mean that it will not ever happen to you. Be careful whom you let into your property. Once in, it is difficult and time-consuming to get tenants out, and there is little you can do, physically, to stop them damaging your property while they are in occupation.

By and large, there are many more good tenants 'out there' than bad. You need to develop techniques to ensure that the bad tenants in your properties are kept to a minimum.

Ideally, you will be looking for a tenant with a permanent job who will look after the property and will want to stay there for a long time. Long-term lets are preferable because this reduces the costs of letting and periods of time when the property is empty (when you will not be receiving rent).

A landlord says ...

'It is better to have a good tenant paying £300 per month than a bad tenant paying £350.'

References

The main types of references are employer's, bank, previous landlords', and character references.

The employer's reference is the most important as it gives some assurance that the tenant will be able to pay the rent. Remember that the applicant's current landlord's reference may not tell you the whole picture if the landlord is anxious for the tenant to leave, and character references can be unreliable (beware the reference which is too glowing – it is probably fictitious).

You should look for tenants with a good employment history. If the tenant has had frequent job changes in the past, this trend will probably continue, and he is less likely to stay in the property for any length of time.

References are particularly important for the more expensive properties, where they should be taken as a matter of course. However, for HMOs, many landlords do not take references and go by their own judgment. HMO tenants are usually in a hurry and are not prepared to wait for the time it would take for the landlord to obtain a reference. If there is any delay, they may well go elsewhere.

A landlord says ...

'Do not trust fulsome character references – they are usually untrue.'

Credit reference agencies

These are usually fairly cheap and very useful; for example, they will pick up on the tenant who has County court judgments registered against them. Your landlords' association will usually be able to suggest a suitable company and many of the online landlord sites will also advertise credit reference agencies for landlords. If you are a member of a landlords' association, it may have a special arrangement with a company which will offer special rates to members.

Tip

When doing a company let, check that it is a genuine company. You can do a basic company search for free on the Companies House website (see the Appendix).

'Gut' feeling

This is often the best way of deciding whether a tenant will be suitable or not. It is a skill which develops with experience. Every landlord will have their own idiosyncrasies, and preferences and prejudices when choosing tenants. There follow some comments from experienced landlords on how they chose their tenants.

> Never let a property to someone who comes to you desperate for immediate accommodation, particularly if it is late at night. These people will almost always turn out to be nightmare tenants.

> A person with a cheerful, friendly disposition, and who has a sense of humour, is more likely to be a good tenant than someone who is grumpy and miserable.

> Do not be prejudiced against Housing Benefit tenants. It is more important to consider the type of people they are.

A landlord says ...

'If in doubt, keep them out.'

Comments from HMO landlords:

> I never let to a tenant who is bigger and meaner looking than me.

> Beware of the tenant who, when you ask him where he is living at the moment, says, 'I am staying round a mates".

If people do not tell you where they are coming from or give you any personal information, don't let them in. There is almost always a problem past.

I have generally found that foreigners and people from ethnic minorities make very good tenants. They are more respectful than many English people and usually would not dream of leaving a flat in a mess.

Do not be prejudiced against a tenant's looks. Be aware of different cultures and age groups. Remember, con men are always well dressed and appear respectable.

Choosing a good tenant is particularly important for high-rental properties, as the inevitable delay in obtaining an eviction order may result in large losses. If a landlord is uncertain about the tenant's ability to pay the rent, he should take security in the form of a guarantee. However, careful checks should also be carried out against the guarantor, as there is no point in taking a guarantee from someone unless he is financially in a position to make good any losses caused by the tenant.

Tip

Be wary of letting tenants who take tenancy agreements away to get them signed by guarantors. It is not unknown for them to forge the guarantor's signature! Ensure that the guarantor signs in front of you or have the signature witnessed by someone you can trust.

It is sometimes possible to let property on a long-term basis to companies for housing asylum seekers. If you are interested in this, you can obtain further information from your local landlords' association. Many local authorities are now setting up schemes whereby they will lease a property for a period of years (often five) to use for housing homeless families. You will normally receive a rent which is slightly less than the market rate, but you are assured a regular rent for that period and the local authority is responsible for the maintenance of the property. Contact the Housing Officer of your local authority for more information.

Sample tenant's letter of authority to Housing Benefit Office

John Smith
123 Any Street
Anytown
ANY 456

The Housing Benefit Office
Anytown Town Hall
Anyshire
ANY 123

Dear Sirs

Re: 456 Other Street, Anytown, ANY 789

I hereby authorise and request you to provide my landlord Arthur Rigby at 111 North Street, Anytown, ANY 999 any information he may request regarding my application for Housing Benefit and any other information he may request regarding my Housing Benefit entitlement and payment of Housing Benefit to me after my application has been processed. I also authorise you to provide details of previous applications for Housing Benefit if these are going to affect the rent paid to my current landlord.

I hereby request that Housing Benefit is paid direct to my landlord at 111 North Street, Anytown, ANY 999.

Yours faithfully

Signed ....*JJ Smith*.......... Dated ....*14 June 2005*...........
        JOHN JAMES SMITH

Include this paragraph if you, as landlord, want the benefit to be paid directly to you.

Housing Benefit tenants

If a tenant is on benefit, he may be entitled to have all or part of his rent paid by Housing Benefit. There are many problems associated with Housing Benefit and many landlords have a policy of not letting to Housing Benefit tenants, although in some localities landlords will have little choice. However, provided you are careful when selecting tenants, they can be profitable and problem-free.

When a new Housing Benefit tenant is taken on, there is much that the landlord can do to help speed up the process. Housing Benefit Offices are often accused of unwarranted delays; however, these are sometimes because they are still missing some of the information they need before the application can be processed. It is important for your cash flow that payment is made to you as quickly as possible. Also, if there are long delays resulting in a large sum being sent to the tenant at a later stage, there is a great temptation for the tenant to spend it (rather than give it to you). The following points will help you:

- The application should go in well before the tenant is due to move into the property. Housing Benefit cannot normally be backdated to before an application is made.

- Under the verification framework, Housing Benefit Officers will need to see original documents. In particular, they will need to see the original tenancy agreement. Ensure that these are sent to the Housing Benefit Office promptly.

- Tenants should be asked to sign a letter of authority (see sample letter on previous page) authorising the Housing Benefit Office to provide information to the landlord. If this is not done, the Housing Benefit Officers will not be able to give any information to the landlord about the progress of the tenant's application, even if they want to, because of the Data Protection Act.

- If you regularly let to Housing Benefit tenants, you may wish to consider keeping a stock of the claim forms to give them.

- Some tenants, particularly those who find writing difficult or whose first language is not English, may appreciate your help in filling in the application form. If you do this, you will at least have the security of knowing that the form has actually been completed and submitted! Remember that if you fill in the form for the tenant, you have to state on the form that you have done this.

- The form asks that where the rent includes services (such as water rates, heating, and cleaning), it should be stated how much of the rent figure is in respect of each of these. There are government guidelines as to how much can be paid (if anything) in respect of each type of service. However, if the Benefit Office is provided with suitable original evidence, it might be able to depart from these guidelines. If you are able to assist your tenant by providing this information, this will help speed up his application considerably.

- If your property is an HMO, make sure that each individual unit can be identified (e.g. by giving a room number). Try not to change these numbers as otherwise this can cause problems at the Housing Benefit Office and may cause it to stop payment of the benefit, if the change makes it appear as if the same room is being claimed for twice.

- Remember that Housing Benefit will be limited to the allowable rent for a unit of a suitable size for the applicant. For example, a single parent with a child needs a two-bedroomed property. If he claims in respect of a three-bedroomed property, he will normally only receive Housing Benefit to the value of a two-bedroomed property and will have to find the difference himself. This situation may lead to arrears building up. This should be borne in mind when renting to Housing Benefit tenants.

- It is possible for tenants to apply to the Rent Officer and ask him to advise in advance the rent figure that will be used as a starting point for working out their Housing Benefit entitlement.

All applications for Housing Benefit for private rented properties are referred to a Rent Officer for determination. This is described in the separate section on the Rent Service, see below.

Tip

Ensure that the letter of authority which the tenant signs authorises the Benefit Office to discuss previous benefit claims with you, as well as the current claim.

Even if you and your tenant are meticulous in filing the correct documentation to the Benefit Office in good time, you may still experience very long delays before payment is made. The length of the delay varies across the county, but unfortunately in some areas it has reached a level which many landlords find unacceptable. If this is the case in your area, there is little you can do, other than refuse to take Housing Benefit tenants. New landlords and landlords buying property in a new area should make enquiries about this before accepting tenants on benefit. Your local landlords' association is a good source of information about this.

Housing Benefit claw-back

One of the advantages of letting to Housing Benefit tenants at present is that their rent can be paid to you directly by the Housing Benefit Office. This means that you get paid regularly and the tenant is not tempted to spend his rent cheque on other things. However, one potential problem with this is that if the Housing Benefit Office discovers that an overpayment of benefit has been made to a previous landlord of the tenant, even in respect of a completely different property in another part of the country, it can deduct the overpayment from rent paid to the current landlord. It is difficult for a landlord to prevent this happening as, strictly speaking, the Housing Benefit is a benefit due to the tenant, not the landlord, whose contractual relationship is with the tenant, not the Housing Benefit Office, although the payment can be made directly to the landlord. There are several things landlords can do to protect themselves from Housing Benefit claw-back:

- Check all new Housing Benefit tenants very carefully and take a reference from their previous landlord. This sort of problem is more likely to occur with the less 'respectable' type of tenants, particularly if they move frequently from one property to another.

- Visit the property regularly so that you can advise the Benefit Office if the tenant has vacated or if there are any other changes in his circumstances that affect his benefit (so there will not be an overpayment to you).

- If you are concerned that there may have been a previous overpayment to the tenant, insist that the rent is paid to you by the tenant, rather than paid directly to you by the Benefit Office. The Benefit Office can only claw back from the landlord rent that has been paid to the landlord direct.

- Join your local landlords' association. Sometimes it has a protocol agreement regarding the circumstances in which a claw-back can be recovered from a landlord.

- If a claim is made against you for a claw-back, check that any paperwork served on you by the Benefit Office requesting a repayment is correct (if it is not, it may not be entitled to repayment). Your local landlords' association will be able to advise you here.

Note that under regulations which came into effect in October 2001, if a landlord reports (in writing) a suspected overpayment to the Housing Benefit Office, and it is found that the tenant has either made a fraudulent claim or has deliberately failed to report a change in circumstances, the overpayment will not now be claimed back from the landlord, provided the landlord has not colluded with the tenant in obtaining the overpayment.

Local Housing Allowance

At the time of writing, a new Housing Benefit regime is gradually being rolled out across the country. This will involve the introduction of standard Local Housing Allowances for private rentals. This will be a flat rate which will be paid based on the rent to which the tenant will be entitled. If the tenant's property has a higher rent, he will be responsible for the extra money and if he finds a cheaper property, he can keep the difference. The housing allowance will be paid directly to the tenant as standard, and it will only be possible for it to be paid directly to the landlord or letting agent if the tenant is deemed to be 'vulnerable'. The landlord can also, as it is now, ask for the benefit to be paid directly if the tenant is eight weeks or more in arrears.

Further details of the new system can be found on the Department for Work and Pensions' website at www.dwp.gov.uk/housingbenefit. It is hoped that this system will be simpler and less costly and time-consuming to administer.

Generally

Try to keep on good terms with your local Housing Benefit Office, particularly if you have several tenants who are on benefit. If you are considerate and helpful towards the Office, it is more likely to reciprocate. Remember also that the landlord has a duty to the Benefit Office, if rent is being paid directly, to keep it informed, in particular if the tenant vacates the property or is absent for a long period. You should also let the Officer know if you become aware of any other circumstances which may affect the benefit, such as the birth of a child, someone else moving into the property, or the tenant getting a job.

The Rent Service and the assessment of rent for Housing Benefit

The Rent Service (formerly the Rent Officer Service) was started in 1965. It is now an Executive Agency of the Office of the Deputy Prime Minister, and nationally funded.

The Rent Service work centres mainly around the private rented housing sector in England. Currently it:

- carries out rental valuations for Housing Benefit purposes, i.e. to determine whether Housing Benefit claimants (and prospective claimants) are being asked to pay more rent than their landlords might reasonably be expected to obtain in open market conditions;

- makes fair rent determinations;

- advises local authorities about the effects on rent of housing renovation grant applications by landlords; and

- carries out rental valuations and provide information, on a more informal basis, for a variety of customers within the public and private sector.

The service has a huge database of market rents that is regularly updated from information provided by private landlords, letting agencies and other sources, and this is used extensively in its work.

Housing Benefit valuations

When an application is made for benefit, the local authority passes this over to the Rent Service, which will consider the form, and value the property. Sometimes it is possible to provide a valuation without an inspection, for example if the property has been inspected previously. However, if the property is unusual or if the Rent Officer thinks it needs looking at, he will visit the property to make an inspection.

When inspecting the property, the Rent Officer will be looking at four basic factors: the age of the property, its location, its size and its condition. Of course, the only one of these that the landlord has any control over is the condition. Any aspect of the condition that directly affects living in the property will affect the valuation.

Negative aspects can be damp, rotten or old windows, a leaking roof, lack of adequate insulation, or lack of one of the basic facilities.

Positive aspects can be improvement by double glazing, central heating and having a garage or car parking space (particularly in city locations).

Cosmetic aspects of the property, such as decoration, will be less important. If the property is furnished, the officer will be looking to see that the quality of the furniture is reasonable. So there is little point in furnishing a property for Housing Benefit tenants with antiques!

After inspection, the Rent Officer will determine the 'claim-related rent', which is based on his valuation of the property or an equivalent of the right size. The Rent Officer will also give the 'local reference rent', which consists of average figures (updated monthly) held by the Rent Office relating to the different types of property for different areas. Often a valuation will be limited to the relevant local reference rent, and a property in good condition will not achieve, for benefit purposes, the open market rent.

Both figures are then sent back to the local authority, and it will base the benefit paid on the lower figure, taking into account the particular circumstances of the claimant. However, it is rare for the benefit paid to be greater than the claim-related rent, as any difference will have to come out of the local authority's own budget. It is generally only prepared to do this in special circumstances, such as where the claimant is in some way vulnerable.

If there is any difference between the benefit paid and the contractual rent, the tenant will still be liable for the balance, and will have to pay this to the landlord himself.

Occasionally, the rent as assessed by the Rent Service is challenged. If this happens, the Rent Officer will send the papers to the redetermination unit at Leeds which will look at the case afresh.

As well as dealing with claims, the Rent Office also sends to the local authority monthly 'indicative rent levels' for the various categories of property. These are to allow the local authority to make interim benefit payments if there is any delay in getting the claim-related rent figure from the Rent Office.

As far as the new Local Housing Allowances are concerned, these will be set by the Rent Service towards the end of the month before they become applicable. They will be reviewed monthly. The Rent Service will pass the rates to the local authority just before the start of the month to which they apply and the local authority will publicise them in a way that is accessible to landlords and tenants (e.g. in its reception area, the local paper or on its website).

The Rent Service is a public service and Rent Officers are usually prepared to give information to anyone who makes an enquiry about local rent levels in the area, current local reference rents and any other information that may be helpful. They cannot, however, give specific advice about rent for individual properties.

For more information about the Rent Service, see its website at www.the rentservice.gov.uk.

CHAPTER 5

The agreement

Why and when is it necessary?

Although it is not strictly necessary to create a valid assured shorthold tenancy (AST) in England & Wales, all landlords should ensure that their tenants have signed a written tenancy agreement prior to going into possession. However, do note that in Scotland it is necessary to have a written tenancy agreement for it to be a short assured tenancy (SAT).

Informal oral arrangements can be a recipe for disaster:

- If a tenancy is oral, there may be arguments later about its terms, even if these were clearly discussed when the tenant went in.

- Once a tenant is in occupation, you cannot then force him to sign an agreement that varies the terms of his tenancy, so it is essential that this is done before he goes in.

- The landlord will need a formal agreement so he can insert clauses that will protect his position (see below) and regulate the tenant's use of the property.

- You will not be able to use the accelerated possession procedure (see chapter 7) to evict the tenant, where there is no written tenancy agreement.

- If no written tenancy agreement is provided, a landlord is required by law to provide the tenant with written details of the main terms of his tenancy within six months; so he might as well provide a proper written tenancy agreement to begin with.

Although all tenancies should have a formal written tenancy agreement, this is not always essential with licences. For example, it may not always be necessary in the following circumstances:

- Letting a room in your house to lodgers.

- Bed-and-breakfast accommodation.

However, even if a formal letting agreement is not provided in these circumstances, there should always be some paperwork to prove the terms of the letting, in case there is a dispute at a later date.

A landlord says ...

'Do not let a tenant in until the paperwork is signed.'

The Unfair Terms in Consumer Contracts Regulations 1999

These will be referred to in this book as the Unfair Terms Regulations. These regulations are the result of an EU directive which initially came into effect in July 1995; they were subsequently redrafted and the updated regulations came into effect on 1 October 1999.

These regulations apply to all contracts which involve a 'consumer' (i.e. an individual not acting for the purposes of his business or profession) and a 'seller or supplier' (whose definition includes most landlords). They were designed to prevent consumers being placed at a disadvantage when signing formal contracts with large organisations, whose contracts normally include standard terms and conditions in small print. As everyone knows, these standard terms and conditions are rarely read by the consumer before signing the contract, and even if they are, he has no power to change them. The regulations provide that the consumer will not be bound by a standard term in such a contract if that term is 'unfair'.

These regulations apply to most tenancy agreements, as a landlord will generally be deemed to be acting in the course of a business. They will not apply to landlords who are simply letting their own home (e.g. during a year abroad) if they deal with the letting themselves; however, they will apply to all properties let through letting agents if the agent's standard form of tenancy agreement is used. They will not apply, though, to lettings to another business, for example company lets.

The regulations do not cover what are called 'core terms'. These are terms setting the price (i.e. the rent) and terms defining the subject matter of the contract (i.e. describing the property to be let). They may, however, apply to rent review clauses. A standard term is unfair if it creates a significant imbalance in the parties' rights and obligations under the contract, to the detriment of the consumer, and contrary to the requirement of good faith. The regulations are aimed at terms which have the effect of reducing the consumers' rights under the ordinary rules of contract or the general law. The regulations also require that plain and intelligible language is used and a term is open to challenge if it is difficult to understand by the ordinary person. The requirement of plain language applies to all terms, including core terms.

The fact that one term in an agreement has been found unfair does not affect the validity of the rest of the agreement. It is just that clause which will be unenforceable.

Consumers (or tenants) who have a complaint about a contract term can refer it to their local Trading Standards Office, which may in turn refer it to the Unfair Contract Terms Unit at the Office of Fair Trading (whose address is in the Appendix). However, the main effect of an unfair term is that it is void and will not be enforced by a court in legal proceedings. So if rent is increased by a rent review term which is found to be unfair, a landlord will not be able to obtain a County court judgment in respect of the unpaid excess rent or obtain a possession order on the grounds of those rent arrears. He will also probably face an order to pay the tenant's legal costs.

In November 2001 the Office of Fair Trading (OFT) issued a document called *Guidance on Unfair Terms in Tenancy Agreements* and this needs to be considered when drafting tenancy agreements. It can be bought from the OFT or downloaded for free from its website at www.oft.gov.uk. This is discussed in the sections below, where it is referred to as the 'OFT guidance'.

It is, however, perhaps worth making a few general comments. Any clauses which limit or exclude rights which tenants would otherwise have had are almost certainly going to breach the regulations and be deemed unfair, unless there is a very good reason for them (which should be apparent from the agreement). Clauses which impose any penalty or charge on the tenant must provide that the charge be both reasonable in amount and reasonably incurred. Where a clause states that a tenant may only do something with the landlord's written consent, this should be followed by the words '(consent not to be unreasonably withheld)' or similar. Finally, any clauses which are difficult to understand or which use legal terminology which is not in common use, will also be vulnerable to being found invalid under the regulations.

Individual terms you will need in the agreement

Essential terms

Details of the following information **must** be provided by the landlord to the tenant whether there is a written tenancy agreement or not. It is a criminal offence for a landlord to fail to provide this information to a tenant within 28 days of a request (unless he has a reasonable excuse, such as being on holiday).

The tenancy's commencement date

It is important that the tenancy is dated and that it is clear from the document, the date on which the tenancy started. As set out in chapter 1, the law governing a tenancy depends upon when the tenancy was initially granted. There may be new laws in the future which affect tenants' rights. If the tenancy goes on a long time, it may become difficult to prove exactly when the tenancy started if this is not set out in the agreement. For this reason you should always keep a copy of the first tenancy agreement, even if subsequent agreements are given to the tenant. Regarding the subsequent agreements, they should, of course, also be kept.

You will need to know the precise date the current or last fixed term started, for working out when the fixed term ends, and the days in the month or week when subsequent periodic tenancies begin and end. This information is necessary if you have to serve any Section 21 notices (Section 33 notices in Scotland). (For notices requiring possession, see chapter 8.)

The commencement date of a tenancy is also important for working out what day in the week or month the rent runs from. Normally rent is payable on the day of the month or week which is the anniversary of the commencement date (e.g. if the tenancy started on Monday 3 January, a monthly rent will fall due on the third day of every subsequent month and weekly rent will fall due every Monday). Landlords who let several properties usually like all rent to be paid on the same day, usually the first of the month, and if so, the agreement should stipulate that rent is payable on that day. To prevent confusion, it might be wise in this case for the agreement to provide for the tenant to pay an irregular amount for the first month (calculated on a daily basis) so that the rent will run from the stipulated payment day, if the tenancy actually commenced on another day. So if the tenancy starts on 20 January, the tenant will pay 12 days' rent up to 31 January and then the full month's rent on the first day of every month thereafter.

The term

It is normal practice for a tenancy agreement to be for a fixed term, and the most common fixed term is six months. In Scotland, the tenancy agreement must be for at least six months to be a SAT. The legal effect of a fixed term is that you cannot evict the tenant (other than under the 'bad tenant' grounds – see chapter 8) and the tenant is liable for the rent, for its duration. So if in a six-month term the tenant moves out after four months, you can still claim the remaining two months rent from him, unless you relet the property to someone else after he has gone or if you end the fixed term by agreement with the tenant. However, the OFT guidance considers that it is unfair to prevent a tenant from ending or assigning a tenancy if there is another suitable tenant available to take his place; see further on this below.

It is wise when letting to new tenants not to make the term too long. Tenants are not always as satisfactory as they seem when you initially interview them. For example, they may continually pay late, causing administration problems, or you may receive complaints about their behaviour from neighbours. If you have a six-month AST you can simply serve a notice requiring possession on them to expire at the end of the six-month period and then if they fail to move out, you can evict them (see chapter 8). The tenants may object to this but there is nothing they can do about it. However, if you have given them a 12-month tenancy, you will have to wait until the end of the 12 months to get them out. If the tenants prove satisfactory, they can always stay on at the property at the end of the term, either under a new fixed-term agreement or under a periodic tenancy.

Another reason for going for a six-month tenancy is that in an AST the tenant has the right to refer the rent to the Rent Assessment Committee during the first six months. If the Committee decides to fix a new rent, this will apply to the whole of the fixed term, even if there is a rent review clause in the agreement.

Note

Most local authority accreditation schemes provide for tenancies to be for a period of one year, particularly if your property is to be used to house homeless families referred to you by the local authority.

The rent

It is important that there is no dispute over the rent. The amount should clearly be stated in the agreement, together with the period of payment. It is generally best to make this monthly, as most people get paid monthly now. However, for some houses in multiple occupation (HMO) properties you may feel it best to collect rent weekly on the basis that the tenants are likely to be more able and willing to pay smaller weekly sums than larger monthly ones. You should in all agreements specify that the rent is payable in advance, otherwise the law will imply that it is payable in arrears. You can also set out in the agreement the method the rent is to be paid, for example by standing order into a specified bank account. For a discussion about when the date rent should be paid, see the paragraph on the commencement date above.

If rent is to be paid weekly, the landlord is required by law to provide the tenant with a rent book, available from Lawpack.

Tip

You should never allow a tenant the possession of a property until the payments for the first month's rent and the damage deposit have cleared through your bank. No exceptions should be made to this rule.

Other important terms

The following are other important terms, most of which should always be included in the agreement. However, unlike the terms above, you will not be potentially liable under criminal law if they are omitted.

A description of the property

This sounds obvious, but you should be careful to define the property accurately. If the tenancy agreement is for a room in a shared house, for example, make sure that all the rooms have names or numbers (and do not change them). Flats should be clearly described: first floor or ground floor, etc. – again it is a good idea to number them. You should also make it clear if any part of the property is excluded. For example, in a large property with outbuildings, some of these might be separately let as garages to neighbours or used to store your own property. The agreement should make it clear which of these are part of the letting and which are excluded. If the letting includes a parking space or garage, this should also be mentioned. This is particularly important for flats which all have their own parking space adjacent to the property (consider marking and numbering the parking bays).

Payments other than rent

The agreement should make it quite clear which payments will be made by the tenant and which by the landlord. For example:

- **Council Tax** – this will usually be payable by the tenant, but for HMOs it is normally payable by the landlord.

- **Water charges** – if there is no express provision, then they will be the tenant's responsibility. However, often the landlord will accept responsibility. Landlords should be wary of this though if the supply is metered.

- **Utilities** – for ASTs and assured tenancies (ATs), these are almost invariably paid by the tenant. However, in house-sharing arrangements, they may be paid by the landlord, particularly if he is a resident landlord.

For all payments where the landlord is responsible, the agreement should provide for the rent to be increased if the payments are increased, so the landlord is not out of pocket.

Tip

If utilities are to be in the tenant's name, it is best to arrange this before he moves in.

Penalty clauses

Tenancy agreements (particularly those drafted by some letting agents) sometimes include stringent penalty clauses, for example for late payment of rent. However, these are now liable to be found void under the Unfair Terms Regulations and a landlord needs to be careful when using them. The following are examples of clauses that are often used:

- A clause providing for interest on late payment of rent. This is a standard clause. Unless the rate of interest is excessive, this will not fall foul of the regulations. Indeed, this type of clause is recommended, otherwise a landlord will only be able to claim interest on unpaid rent if he brings court proceedings. A typical clause of this type will provide for interest to be paid at three or four per cent above the bank base rate.

- A clause providing for a fixed penalty for non-payment of rent. If this is used instead of an interest clause and is for a modest sum, then it will probably be found to be fair, if challenged. A landlord could justifiably say that it was to make the agreement clearer and to get rid of complicated interest calculations. However, if it is in addition to an interest clause and/or is for a punitive amount (e.g. £5 per day), it may not be upheld.

- Clauses providing for fixed fees for administration expenses; for example, stating that charges of £X will be charged per occasion when rent is paid other than in the manner specified in the agreement (e.g. not by standing order); stating that £X will be charged every time the property is visited to collect or pursue late rent or every time a letter is sent demanding unpaid rent; stating that £X will be charged every time an appointment is missed. If these clauses reflect a genuine expense that the landlord will incur, then they may be reasonable. However, if they are in the nature of a penalty, they are vulnerable to challenge. For example, a 'missed appointments' clause would be fair if it was charged in respect of missed appointments made at the tenant's request and if the sum charged genuinely reflected the landlord's expenses.

If it is important to the landlord that a clause of this nature (other than a standard clause for interest) is included in the tenancy agreement, it would be wise to specifically draw it to the attention of the tenant at the time he signs the agreement and explain it to him. If he agrees to it, you should ask him to initial the clause in the agreement. This would give the landlord some protection if the tenant subsequently challenges the clause.

Note

Any unusual clauses in the agreement should be given prominence (e.g. by having them in bold type).

The deposit

You should always take a deposit from tenants and the agreement should specify the amount of the deposit and how it is to be used. There are probably more disputes about damage deposits than anything else; landlords complain that tenants leave owing rent equal to or more than the value of the deposit so they are out of pocket if there are repairs needed, and tenants complain that landlords routinely retain deposits without good cause. It is usually very important to tenants that deposits are returned, as they need the money to pay the deposit for their next rented property.

Your agreement should therefore be very clear about deposits and should deal with the following points:

- The amount of the deposit. It is usual for this to be the equivalent of one month's rent. It should not be for more than two months' rent, otherwise it will be held to be a premium, which is inadvisable.

- What the landlord can use the deposit for (e.g. damage to the premises or furniture, unpaid rent and services) and also any sum repayable to the local authority when Housing Benefit has been paid directly to the landlord.

- A requirement that a tenant should make up the deposit if the landlord has to use part of it during the tenancy (e.g. for repairs).

- Whether the tenant shall be entitled to interest on the deposit (normally the agreement provides that interest will not be paid).

- When the deposit is to be returned to the tenant – normally this is when the tenant gives up possession of the property; however, it is a good idea for the agreement to provide that if the tenant's Housing Benefit has been paid directly to the landlord, the landlord is entitled to hold the deposit until he is sure that there will be no claw-back. He can, however, only retain the deposit for a reasonable period of time.

- The agreement should also state that the tenant is not entitled to withhold rent on the grounds that the landlord is holding a deposit. However, be warned that this will not always stop a tenant from leaving without paying his last month's rent!

There are often misunderstandings about the way deposits should be dealt with, particularly when proceedings are being brought for possession on the basis of rent arrears. While the tenant is in the property, the deposit is held by the landlord as security and should not be credited to the tenant against unpaid rent. When the tenant leaves, the landlord will inspect the property, and assess its condition. The damage deposit should then be used as follows:

1. If there are any repairs that need to be done or items to be replaced, the cost of this will be deducted from the deposit. It may also be necessary to clean the property and again the costs of this will normally be deducted. It should be emphasised that costs must be

reasonable and landlords should keep all receipts. There may be other deductions that are appropriate (e.g. if there has been a local authority claw-back). However, all deductions from the deposit must be authorised by the relevant clause in the tenancy agreement.

2. After these costs have been deducted, and only after this, the remaining money is credited to any rent arrears due.

3. The balance (if any) is then paid to the tenant.

Note that the landlord cannot claim for damage caused by 'fair wear and tear', i.e. a normal consequence of the tenant living in and using the property.

Ideally, the landlord will inspect the property with the tenant (who will not be in arrears) the day the tenant leaves, the property will be in perfect condition, and the landlord will hand the deposit back there and then. If there are deductions that need to be made, you should deal with any work quickly so as not to delay returning any remaining balance to the tenant.

The Housing Act 2004 provides for a mandatory tenancy deposit scheme, although the relevant clauses of the Act have not come into force at the time of writing this book. It is possible that any scheme introduced will be based on the current tenancy deposit scheme which has been introduced by the Association of Residential Letting Agents (ARLA) for its regulated agents. More information can be found on the scheme's website at www.tds.gb.com. Do note that this does not apply in Scotland.

Tip

If you are using a letting agent, make sure that he has a client's money protection scheme, as damage deposits held by him will be at risk if he goes out of business. If this happens, you will still be responsible for paying the money back to the tenant.

Tip

Many local authorities have damage deposit guarantee schemes to help people obtain housing in the private sector, who otherwise could not raise the initial payments.

Rent review

As set out in chapter 7, you can normally only increase the rent either by agreement (usually by the tenant signing a new tenancy agreement at an increased rent) or by serving a notice of increase. But a tenant may refuse to sign a new tenancy agreement and new rents in notices of increase can be referred to the Rent Assessment Committee. Rent usually cannot be increased at all during the fixed term. These potential problems can be overcome by including a clause providing for rent review in the tenancy agreement. It is important that this clause is as clear as possible and that any mechanism for calculating any new rent is easily understood and fair, to prevent the clause falling foul of the unfair terms in consumer contracts regulations.

There are different types of rent review clause. Some of them provide a mechanism for rent to be increased at specified periods by way of reference to a government index, such as the Retail Price Index. Others simply provide for the landlord to increase the rent at specified periods, but allow the tenant to give notice to terminate the agreement if he does not agree to it. Note that in a recent case where a rent review clause in a tenancy agreement provided for the landlord to increase the rent substantially (from £4,680 pa to £25,000 pa), the Court of Appeal found that this clause was invalid, as it was merely a 'device' to allow the landlord to repossess the property (on the basis of rent arrears – the tenant could not pay the increased rent) and thus avoid the provisions of the Housing Act 1988; it was not a genuine provision for the increase of rent.

Most standard tenancy agreements, however, do not include rent review clauses, because if a tenancy is a short (e.g. six-month) AST, the landlord can simply serve a Section 21 notice (Section 33 notice in Scotland) and evict the tenant if he refuses to sign a new agreement at a higher rent.

Repairs and redecoration

Most landlords have statutory repairing obligations which they cannot contract out of (see chapters 4 and 7), but the agreement should state who is responsible for non-structural repairs and redecoration, which are not covered by statute. However, you will not wish your tenant to redecorate the property by painting all the walls black, so it is usual to include a clause either prohibiting him from doing any redecoration at all without the landlord's written permission or from redecorating in anything other than the existing style and colours. If the property includes a garden, the agreement should include a clause requiring the tenant to maintain it. Alternatively, you may wish the agreement to provide for access for your gardener (his charges to be included in the rent).

Note

All clauses forbidding a tenant to do something (e.g. redecorate) must be qualified by including after the prohibition the words 'without the written consent of the Landlord (which will not be withheld unreasonably)' or similar. This will prevent the clause from being invalid under the Unfair Terms Regulations.

Damage and alterations

The law prohibits tenants from deliberately damaging the property, and it is normal for this to be specifically set out in the agreement. Usually there are separate clauses relating to the property and its furniture. The law, however, does not prohibit 'improvements' and therefore the agreement should specifically prohibit any alterations to the property, unless the landlord's written consent is obtained in advance. It is also a good idea to include a separate clause prohibiting the tenant from changing the locks and authorising you to retain a set of keys (for access in the case of emergency).

Use

As the law allows a tenant to use the property for whatever purpose he wants, it is advisable to include a clause restricting use of the property to that of a single, private, residential dwelling, and to include clauses forbidding antisocial behaviour (i.e. causing a nuisance to other tenants and neighbours).

Access

The agreement should specify that the landlord (or his agent) should be permitted to enter and inspect the property upon giving reasonable notice in writing (say 48 hours) to the tenant, but it should also state that in cases of real emergency this requirement will not apply. This is important, as you will need access to carry out regular inspections, do any repairs and to have the annual gas safety checks done. Note, however, that you cannot enter the property if the tenant does not consent, even if you wish to enter for an authorised purpose (such as a gas safety check). If you do this, it can be deemed harassment, which is a criminal offence.

A landlord says ...

'The worst thing about being a landlord is tenants ringing in the middle of the night because they have lost their keys.'

Assignment and subletting

Assignment is where ownership of the tenancy agreement as a whole is transferred from one person to another; subletting is where part or all of the property is let under a separate agreement.

It is essential that there are express covenants against assignment and subletting, as there is little point in carefully vetting your tenants if they can then assign or sublet to whoever they wish. In its guidance, the OFT, however, stated that it considered that an absolute prohibition against assignment could be unfair, as this could force the tenant to pay rent for a property which he may no longer need; for example, if he has to move elsewhere for his job, even though there is someone willing to take the tenancy on. I take the view though that the OFT's point can be adequately met by allowing the tenant to end the tenancy early if a suitable tenant can be found, provided the landlord's reasonable expenses are paid. The landlord can then grant a new tenancy to the replacement. This, to my mind, is a better solution than allowing assignment, which simply adds an extra layer of complication to the tenancy agreement. The landlord should be able to approve the new tenant, but the agreement should state that his approval should not be withheld unreasonably.

Insurance

The landlord will usually arrange for insurance cover, and the agreement should prohibit the tenant from activity which will affect the validity of the insurance cover and also provide for him to be responsible for any increase in the insurance premiums due to his behaviour. However, the tenant cannot be expected to be able to comply with this if he does not know what behaviour is prohibited by the insurers, so the agreement should also provide for the landlord to let the tenant have a copy of the insurance policy. Alternatively, he can provide the tenant with a summary of the relevant terms. The tenant will usually be responsible for the insurance of his own belongings. For more details about insurance, see chapter 4.

Tenants' property left behind

Tenants often go, leaving items at the property which can cause problems for the landlord. If the landlord throws away property which subsequently turns out to be of value, he may be subject to a claim from the tenant for damages. It is wise, therefore, to include a term in the agreement allowing the landlord to dispose of any items left at the property. However, this clause will need to be carefully drafted as the general law does not allow the landlord simply to take the tenant's belongings for himself or to dispose of them without notice to the tenant. For more information on this, see chapter 8.

Address for service

Under Section 48 of the Landlord and Tenant Act 1987, no rent is lawfully due from a tenant unless and until the landlord has given the tenant notice in writing of an address in England & Wales at which notices (including notices in proceedings) can be served on him. It is best that this notice is included in the tenancy agreement. The address can be the address of the landlord's agent or another contact address. This clause is particularly important for landlords who are resident abroad, which for this purpose includes those owners of property situated in England or Wales who live elsewhere in the UK.

Although it is normal practice and prudent to provide a landlord's contact address in Scotland for Scottish property that is let, it is not a legal requirement.

It is also a good idea to specify that any notices or other documents shall be deemed properly served on the tenant either by being left at the premises or by being sent there by registered post or recorded delivery.

Forfeiture

This is an essential clause, as it allows you to evict the tenant during the fixed term under certain circumstances (e.g. as specified in the Housing Act 1988 or the Housing (Scotland) Act 1988 in Scotland). The actual wording of most standard forfeiture clauses is somewhat misleading as it states that in certain specified circumstances (e.g. if rent is unpaid for 14 days) the landlord can re-enter and the tenancy will be 'determined' (ended). Of course, the landlord cannot physically re-enter the property himself: physical re-entry can only be done by a court bailiff (or Sheriff Officer in Scotland) pursuant to a possession order. This should be made clear as otherwise the clause may fall foul of the Unfair Terms Regulations. However, you should be careful about altering the wording of a forfeiture clause unless you know what you are doing, as you may alter its effect. A suitable form of wording for tenancies in England & Wales would be:

If the Tenant does not pay the rent (or any part) within 21 days of the due date (whether it has been formally demanded or not) or if the Tenant fails to comply with the Tenant's obligations under this Agreement, or if any of the circumstances mentioned in Grounds 2, 8 or 10 to 15 or 17 of Part II of Schedule 2, and in Schedule 2A, to the Housing Act 1988 arise, then the Landlord may, subject to any statutory provisions, recover possession of the Property and the tenancy will come to an end. The Landlord retains all his other rights in respect of the Tenant's obligations under this Agreement. Note – if anyone lives at the Property or if the tenancy is an assured tenancy under the Housing Act 1988, the Landlord cannot recover possession of the Property without a court order. This clause does not affect the Tenant's rights under the Protection from the Eviction Act 1977.

A suitable form of wording for tenancies in Scotland would be:

If the Tenant does not pay the rent (or any part) within 21 days of the due date (whether it has been formally demanded or not) or if the Tenant fails to comply with the Tenant's obligations under this Agreement, or if any of the circumstances mentioned in Grounds 2 and 8 of Part I and Grounds 11, 12, 13, 14, 15 or 16 of Part II of Schedule 5 to the Housing (Scotland) Act 1988 arise, then the Landlord may, subject to any statutory provisions, recover possession of the Property and the tenancy will come to an end. The Landlord retains all his other rights in respect of the Tenant's obligations under this Agreement. Note – if anyone lives at the Property or if the tenancy is an assured tenancy or short assured tenancy under the Housing (Scotland) Act 1988, the Landlord cannot recover possession of the Property without a court order. This clause does not affect the Tenant's rights under the Rent (Scotland) Act 1984.

If the tenancy agreement you are using does not state that the right of re-entry can only be pursuant to a court order, this should be added. This prevents the clause from being misleading.

Other prohibitions, etc.

There is a number of things landlords may not want the tenant to do, which can be set out in the agreement, for example:

- Keeping pets/animals at the property (although this clause must be qualified so as not to unfairly prevent tenants keeping harmless pets, such as goldfish).

- Using heaters which could be dangerous, such as oil or calor gas heaters (although do not just say 'inflammable materials', as this would be considered unfair as it can include a box of matches).

- Leaving rubbish and the tenant's own possessions in the property at the end of the tenancy.

Remember that you have no control over the tenant once he is in the property. The only way you can legally influence how he treats the property is through the tenancy agreement.

Unreasonable prohibitions and stipulations

It is perhaps worth mentioning here that although the landlord is entitled to include reasonable prohibitions and stipulations in the tenancy agreement, unreasonable attempts to control the tenants' behaviour while they are in the property will be deemed invalid under the Unfair Terms Regulations; for example, clauses that require excessive dusting and cleaning (I have seen agreements, for example, where tenants were required to clean kitchen surfaces with bleach after use and wipe down shower curtains) and clauses where tenants are forbidden to have guests overnight (the OFT guidance points out that this could cause difficulty if a daytime visitor fell ill). Other potentially unreasonable clauses are those forbidding moving the furniture, as this would include not moving the chairs.

I have also heard of instances where landlords (often elderly female landlords) regularly visit the property and order their tenants (often young student tenants) to clean and dust more frequently, as the condition of the property does not meet their own personal standards. This would almost certainly be deemed harassment of the tenants, which is a criminal offence, and a landlord who does this could be on the receiving end of a threatening letter from the local authority and even, potentially, a prosecution in the Magistrates' Court. As long as the tenant is not actually harming the fabric of the property, all you can reasonably ask for is that the property is left in a reasonable condition at the end of the tenancy.

Out-of-season holiday accommodation

This is where a property which is let out as a holiday home for part of the year (e.g. in the summer) is let as an ordinary residential letting during the winter months. Landlords of genuine holiday lets have an additional mandatory ground for possession available to them. However, for the ground to be available, the property must have been occupied for holiday purposes at some time during the 12 months prior to the granting of the tenancy and the letting must be for a fixed term of not more than eight months. The letting must be for a fixed term, not a periodic term, which means that a formal tenancy agreement is essential. A notice informing the tenant that this ground will apply must be served at the commencement of the tenancy.

The inventory/schedule of condition

If the property is let furnished, you should prepare a detailed inventory (often also known as a schedule of condition) of the contents which should be attached to the agreement. The inventory should also give details about items, for example whether they are new or damaged, and perhaps with electrical items the date when they were last checked. This will help prevent arguments later about their condition. Separate columns might be useful for items to be ticked at the end (and perhaps the start) of the tenancy. You should include the lampshades, curtains and carpets, plus details of the physical condition of the property, such as the walls, windows, and doors, as these are also covered by the damage deposit. A schedule of condition should also be prepared for unfurnished properties, as this will provide evidence of the condition of the property (e.g. the walls, doors, and carpets) at the start of the tenancy.

The inventory/schedule of condition should ideally be signed by both landlord and tenant. It is a good idea to include a term in the agreement stating that the condition of the premises and its contents will be deemed to be in good order unless the tenant notifies the landlord to the contrary within a specified time period (say five days).

There are professional companies that can provide an inventory service, and you may find this helpful, particularly for a first let or if you have a number of properties. You should look for a firm which is a member of the Association of Independent Inventory Clerks. Your landlords' association should be able to advise you of any local firms.

Tip

You may also consider giving new tenants an information pack about the property. For example, this could contain details about appliances and how to operate them, where the fuse box, gas and electricity meters are, information about fire safety, and the landlord's telephone number to ring in the case of emergency. For holiday properties, landlords could also give details of local amenities.

Guarantees

If you intend to have a guarantor, he can either sign the tenancy agreement itself, in which case it should contain a paragraph specifying the circumstances under which he will become liable, or he can sign a separate form of guarantee. Remember that a guarantor will only be liable for terms that are brought to his attention at the time he signs the guarantee and not for any subsequent terms that may be agreed with the tenant. The guarantor should therefore sign a fresh form of guarantee every time a new agreement is signed by the tenant.

Stamp Duty Land Tax (SDLT)

This is a government tax (formerly just called 'stamp duty') payable on tenancy agreements, which is recorded by a stamp on the document. Since the last Budget, very few new tenancies will now be liable for SDLT. However, SDLT was payable on many tenancy agreements in the past. It is important to note that if you are going to use them in court proceedings, a judge will not accept them as evidence if they have not been stamped. It is important, therefore, that tenancy agreements which are going to be used in possession proceedings are properly stamped, if SDLT is payable. Judges are now picking up on this point and it is most unwise to assume that they will not notice that the tenancy is unstamped.

Tip

Further information about Stamp Duty Land Tax can be obtained from the Inland Revenue helpline (see the Appendix).

Obtaining tenancy agreements

Lawpack produces excellent tenancy agreement forms for use in both England & Wales and in Scotland for a range of circumstances; see the example of Lawpack's *Furnished House and Flat Rental Agreement on an Assured Shorthold Tenancy* on the following pages or visit www.lawpack. co.uk. Landlords' associations often have forms of tenancy agreements available for their members, or forms can be purchased from law stationers, or on the internet (e.g. at the writer's website at www.landlord law.co.uk). If you feel that any special terms are needed for your property, it is best to get a tenancy agreement drafted by a solicitor, rather than adapt one of the standard forms yourself, as it is easy to fall foul of the Unfair Terms Regulations if you do not know what you are doing. Be sure to use a solicitor who specialises in landlord and tenant work.

If you let property regularly or you are a professional landlord, it is essential to get your standard tenancy agreement reviewed by a solicitor every few years, or to buy new forms. Changes in legislation mean that tenancy agreements that are perfectly valid one year can contain clauses which are invalid the next. For example, the effect of the regulations on unfair terms and the OFT's guidance has meant that almost all tenancy agreements current just a few years ago will now almost certainly contain a number of clauses which would be classed as 'unfair'.

Housing law reform

Under current housing law reform proposals being considered by the Law Commission, it will become mandatory for landlords to provide a form of tenancy agreement and if this is not provided, tenants may be entitled to withhold their rent for a period of up to two months until the tenancy agreement has been given to them. The form of tenancy agreements will also be prescribed by statute and will include much of the law relating to tenancies, such as the landlord's repairing obligations and information about the procedure landlords have to follow to obtain a possession order. No doubt these changes will be covered in the press; however, landlords should ensure that they keep informed, for example, by joining a landlords' association, by subscribing to a suitable newsletter or journal, or via the authors online service. Further information about the proposals can be obtained from the Law Commission's website at www.lawcom.gov.uk or from the Law Reform section of the author's website at www.landlordlaw.co.uk.

Completed example of Lawpack's assured shorthold tenancy agreement

F201E

TENANCY AGREEMENT - ENGLAND & WALES
(for a Furnished House or Flat on an Assured Shorthold Tenancy)

The PROPERTY   *Flat B, 14 Gladstone Street, Ashbourne, Derbyshire, DB2 4AX*

The LANDLORD   *RON ROBERTS of 7 Percy St, Ashbourne, Derbyshire, DB2*
of   *5A2 and TIM BOND of 7 Bath Road, Bristol, BS2 3DJ*

The TENANT   *STEVE ROBERTS, JOHN STEEL, AMANDA JAMES,*
and SUSAN SHAW

The TERM   *NINE* ~~weeks~~/months* beginning on   *13th May 2005*

The RENT   £ *600* per ~~week~~/month* payable in advance on the *5th* of each ~~week~~/month*   (*delete as appropriate)

The DEPOSIT   £ *600*

The INVENTORY   means the list of the Landlord's possessions at the Property which has been signed by the Landlord and the Tenant

DATED   *13th May 2005*

SIGNED   *Ron Roberts*
T Bond
(The Landlord)

S Roberts
J Steel
Amanda James
Susan Shaw
(The Tenant)

THIS TENANCY AGREEMENT comprises the particulars detailed above and the terms and conditions printed overleaf whereby the Property is hereby let by the Landlord and taken by the Tenant for the Term at the Rent.

IMPORTANT NOTICE TO LANDLORDS:
(1) The details of 'The LANDLORD' near the top of this Agreement must include an address for the Landlord in England or Wales as well as his/her name or all names in the case of joint Landlords.
(2) Always remember to give the written Notice to Terminate to the Tenant two clear months before the end of the Term.

IMPORTANT NOTICE TO TENANTS:
(1) In general, if you currently occupy this Property under a protected or statutory tenancy and you give it up to take a new tenancy of the same or other accommodation owned by the same Landlord, that tenancy cannot be an Assured Shorthold Tenancy and this Agreement is not appropriate.
(2) If you currently occupy this Property under an Assured Tenancy which is not an Assured Shorthold Tenancy your Landlord is not permitted to grant you an Assured Shorthold Tenancy of this Property or of alternative property.

Completed example of Lawpack's assured shorthold tenancy agreement (continued)

Terms and Conditions

1. This Agreement is intended to create an Assured Shorthold Tenancy as defined in the Housing Act 1988, as amended by the Housing Act 1996, and the provisions for the recovery of possession by the Landlord in that Act apply accordingly. The Tenant understands that the Landlord will be entitled to recover possession of the Property at the end of the Term.

2. The Tenant's obligations:

   2.1 To pay the Rent at the times and in the manner aforesaid.

   2.2 To pay all charges in respect of any electric, gas, water and telephonic or televisual services used at or supplied to the Property and Council Tax or any similar property tax that might be charged in addition to or replacement of it during the Term.

   2.3 To keep the items on the Inventory and the interior of the Property in a good and clean state and condition and not damage or injure the Property or the items on the Inventory (fair wear and tear excepted).

   2.4 To yield up the Property and the items on the Inventory at the end of the Term in the same clean state and condition is/they was/were in at the beginning of the Term (but the Tenant will not be responsible for fair wear and tear caused during normal use of the Property and the items on the Inventory or for any damage covered by and recoverable under the insurance policy effected by the Landlord under clause 3.2).

   2.5 Not make any alteration or addition to the Property nor without the Landlord's prior written consent (consent not be withheld unreasonably) do any redecoration or painting of the Property.

   2.6 Not do anything on or at the Property which:

   (a) may be or become a nuisance or annoyance to any other occupiers of the Property or owners or occupiers of adjoining or nearby premises

   (b) is illegal or immoral

   (c) may in any way affect the validity of the insurance of the Property and the items listed on the Inventory or cause an increase in the premium payable by the Landlord.

   2.7 Not without the Landlord's prior consent (consent not to be withheld unreasonably) allow or keep any pet or any kind of animal at the Property.

   2.8 Not use or occupy the Property in any way whatsoever other than as a private residence.

   2.9 Not assign, sublet, charge or part with or share possession or occupation of the Property.

   2.10 To allow the Landlord or anyone with the Landlord's written permission to enter the Property at reasonable times of the day to inspect its condition and state of repair, carry out any necessary repairs and gas inspections, or during the last month of the Term, show the Property to prospective new tenants, provided the Landlord has given 24 hours' prior written notice (except in emergency).

   2.11 To pay the Landlord's reasonable costs reasonably incurred as a result of any breaches by the tenant of his obligations under this Agreement.

   2.12 To pay interest at the rate of 4% above the Bank of England base rate from time to time prevailing on any rent or other money due from the Tenant under this Agreement which remains unpaid for more than 14 days, interest to be paid from the date the payment fell due until payment.

   2.13 To provide the Landlord with a forwarding address when the tenancy comes to an end and to remove all rubbish and all personal items (including the Tenant's own furniture and equipment) from the Property before leaving.

3. The Landlord's obligations:

   3.1 The Landlord agrees that the Tenant may live in the Property without unreasonable interruption from the Landlord or any person rightfully claiming under or in trust for the Landlord.

   3.2 To insure the Property and the items listed on the Inventory and use all reasonable efforts to arrange for any damage caused by an insured risk to be remedied as soon as possible and to provide a copy of the insurance policy to the Tenant.

   3.3 To keep in repair:

   3.3.1 the structure and exterior of the Property (including drains gutters and external pipes)

   3.3.2 the installations at the Property for the supply of water, gas and electricity and for sanitation (including basins, sinks, baths and sanitary conveniences)

   3.3.3 the installations at the Property for space heating and heating water.

   3.4 But the Landlord will not be required to

   3.4.1 carry out works for which the Tenant is responsible by virtue of his duty to use the Property in a tenant-like manner

   3.4.2 reinstate the Property in the case of damage or destruction if the insurers refuse to pay out the insurance money due to anything the Tenant has done or failed to do

   3.4.3 rebuild or reinstate the Property in the case of destruction or damage of the Property by a risk not covered by the policy of insurance effected by the Landlord.

4. Ending this Agreement

   4.1 The Tenant cannot normally end this Agreement before the end of the Term. However after the first three months of the Term, if the Tenant can find a suitable alternative tenant, and provided this alternative tenant is acceptable to the Landlord (the Landlord's approval not to be unreasonably withheld) the Tenant may give notice to end the tenancy on a date at least one month from the date that such approval is given by the Landlord. On the expiry of such notice, provided that the Tenant pays to the Landlord the reasonable expenses reasonably incurred by the Landlord in granting the necessary approval and in granting any new tenancy to the alternative tenant, the tenancy shall end.

   4.2 If the Tenant stays on after the end of the fixed term, his tenancy will continue but will run from month to month (a 'periodic tenancy'). This periodic tenancy

can be ended by the Tenant giving at least one month's written notice to the Landlord, the notice to expire at the end of a rental period.

   4.3 If at any time

   4.3.1 any part of the Rent is outstanding for 21 days after becoming due (whether formally demanded or not) and/or

   4.3.2 there is any breach, non-observance or non-performance by the Tenant of any covenant or other term of this Agreement which has been notified in writing to the Tenant and the Tenant has failed within a reasonable period of time to remedy the breach and/or pay reasonable compensation to the Landlord for the breach and/or

   4.3.3 any of the grounds set out as Grounds 2, 8 or Grounds 10-15 (inclusive) (which relate to breach of any obligation by a Tenant) contained in the Housing Act 1988 Schedule 2 apply

   the Landlord may recover possession of the Property and this Agreement shall come to an end. The Landlord retains all his other rights in respect of the Tenant's obligations under this Agreement. Note that if anyone is living at the Property or if the tenancy is an Assured or Assured Shorthold Tenancy then the landlord must obtain a court order for possession before re-entering the Property. This clause does not affect the Tenant's rights under the Protection from Eviction Act 1977.

5. The Deposit

   5.1 The Deposit will be held by the Landlord and will be refunded to the Tenant at the end of the Term (however it ends) at the forwarding address provided to the Landlord but less any reasonable deductions properly made by the Landlord to cover any reasonable costs incurred or losses caused to him by any breaches of the obligations in this Agreement by the Tenant. No interest will be payable to the Tenant in respect of the deposit money.

   5.2 The Deposit shall be repayable to the Tenant as soon as reasonably practicable, however the Landlord shall not be bound to return the Deposit until he is satisfied that no money is repayable to the Local Authority if the Tenant has been in receipt of Housing Benefit, and until after he has had a reasonable opportunity to assess the reasonable cost of any repairs required as a result of any breaches of his obligations by the Tenant or other sums properly due to the Landlord under clause 5.1 above. However, the Landlord shall not, save in exceptional circumstances, retain the deposit for more than one month after the end of the tenancy.

   5.3 If at any time during the Term the Landlord is obliged to deduct from the Deposit to satisfy the reasonable costs occasioned by any breaches of the obligations of the Tenant the Tenant shall make such additional payments as are necessary to restore the full amount of the Deposit.

6. Other provisions

   6.1 The Landlord hereby notifies the Tenant under Section 48 of the Landlord & Tenant Act 1987 that any notices (including notices in proceedings) should be served upon the Landlord at the address stated with the name of the Landlord overleaf.

   6.2 For stamp duty purposes, the Landlord and the Tenant confirm that there is no previous agreement to which this Agreement gives effect.

   6.3 The Landlord shall be entitled to have and retain keys to all the doors to the Property but shall not be entitled to use these to enter the Property without the consent of the Tenant (save in an emergency).

   6.4 Any notices or other documents shall be deemed served on the Tenant during the tenancy by either being left at the Property or by being sent to the Tenant at the Property by first-class post. If notices or other documents are served on the Tenant by post they shall be deemed served on the day after posting.

   6.5 Any person other than the Tenant who pays the rent due hereunder or any part thereof to the Landlord shall be deemed to have made such payment as agent for and on behalf of the Tenant which the Landlord shall be entitled to assume without enquiry.

   6.6 Any personal items left behind at the end of the tenancy after the Tenant has vacated (which the Tenant has not removed in accordance with clause 2.13 above) shall be considered abandoned if they have not been removed within 14 days of written notice to the Tenant from the Landlord, or if the Landlord has been unable to trace the Tenant by taking reasonable steps to do so. After this period the Landlord may remove or dispose of the items as he thinks fit. The Tenant shall be liable for the reasonable disposal costs which may be deducted from the proceeds of sale (if any), and the Tenant shall remain liable for any balance. Any net proceeds of the sale will be dealt with in the same way as the Deposit as set out in clause 5.2 above.

   6.7 In the event of damage to or destruction of the Property by any of the risks insured against by the Landlord the Tenant shall be relieved from payment of the Rent to the extent that the Tenant's use and enjoyment of the Property is thereby prevented and from performance of its obligations as to the state and condition of the Property to the extent of and so long as there prevails such damage or destruction (except to the extent that the insurance is prejudiced by any act or default of the Tenant).

   6.8 Where the context so admits:

   6.8.1 The 'Landlord' includes the persons from time to time entitled to receive the Rent.

   6.8.2 The 'Tenant' includes any persons deriving title under the Tenant.

   6.8.3 The 'Property' includes any part or parts of the Property and all of the Landlord's fixtures and fittings at or upon the Property.

   6.8.4 All references to the singular shall include the plural and vice versa and any obligations or liabilities of more than one person shall be joint and several (this means that they will each be liable for all sums due under this Agreement, not just liable for a proportionate part) and an obligation on the part of a party shall include an obligation not to allow or permit the breach of that obligation.

   6.8.5 All references to 'he', 'him' and 'his' shall be taken to include 'she', 'her' and 'hers'.

CHAPTER 6

During the tenancy

The covenant of quiet enjoyment

Every tenancy agreement contains what is called the 'covenant of quiet enjoyment'. This does not just mean that tenants are entitled to a noise-free environment, but that they have the right to live in the property undisturbed. This means not only that they have the right not to be illegally evicted, but also that the landlord should respect their rights and not do anything that will adversely affect their occupation of the property.

The covenant of quiet enjoyment is most commonly invoked to protect tenants whose landlord is trying to 'persuade' them to leave, perhaps because they are not paying the rent or because he wants the property back for his own uses, but is reluctant to go to court for a possession order. For example, such landlords may constantly visit the property, shout threats at the tenant, and interrupt the gas and electricity supply. This sort of behaviour is illegal and can attract both a criminal charge and make the landlord liable for civil proceedings for an injunction and/or damages. However, the covenant for quiet enjoyment can also apply to other matters. For example, it can cover a landlord's failure to comply with his repairing covenants. The example given in the previous chapter of the elderly lady landlord visiting her tenants and ordering them to carry out excessive cleaning would also come under this heading.

It is important, therefore, that landlords ensure that they are complying with all their covenants, including their obligations to keep the property in proper repair (see below), and that they do not intrude on the tenant's privacy. These may conflict, as clearly the landlord will have to go to the property from time to time to carry out his inspections and repairing obligations. Some tenants may object to this and call it harassment (particularly if they are in arrears of rent). If there is a problem of this nature or there is likely to be, then the landlord should take care only to attend at the property by appointment or by the invitation of the tenant. He should never use his keys to enter the property without the tenants' knowledge or permission, other than in cases of genuine emergency. If the tenant objects to the landlord attending to do inspections or carry out repairs, then the landlord cannot enter. This situation is rare, however, and if it occurs, then the landlord should consider whether he should bring proceedings for possession. Note that if the tenant's failure to allow access for repairs is causing the property to deteriorate, this may in itself be a ground for possession, but this should only be used (for the reasons given in chapter 7) if the deterioration is very serious and urgent remedial work is needed.

A landlord who treats his tenants with respect and who complies with his obligations under the tenancy will be protecting himself from any potential claims from his tenants. He will also find it easier to enforce his own rights against the tenants, should this be necessary.

Although a covenant of quiet enjoyment is not implied into licence agreements, licensees have the right to use the property for the purpose for which occupation was granted, which gives them a certain amount of similar protection for the duration of the licence agreement.

Rent matters

The rent book

If the rent is payable weekly, then a landlord has a legal obligation to provide a tenant with a rent book. This must contain certain prescribed information, but rent books can easily be bought at law stationers. Lawpack also produces one (see www.lawpack.co.uk). There is no legal requirement to provide a rent book if rent is paid monthly. Failure to provide a rent book will not prevent rent becoming due from the tenant, but technically the landlord may be rendering himself liable to prosecution (although in practice this is rarely done).

Collecting rent

In most tenancies the rent will be paid by the tenants by standing order. However, many houses in multiple occupation (HMO) tenants do not have bank accounts and will pay cash. For these types of tenants, often the only way the landlord can ensure that he gets paid is to go round and collect the rent personally. Collecting rent is a also good opportunity to inspect the property.

Good times to collect rent are either on Friday afternoons or Sunday mornings. Many people get paid on Friday so this is a good time to catch a tenant before he has had an opportunity to spend it. If a tenant is trying to avoid you, Sunday morning is the most inconvenient time for him to disappear.

Be careful, however, when collecting rent, that you do not lay yourself open to a charge of harassment. Be polite at all times, and never enter the property unless you are invited to do so by the tenant. If a tenant is in arrears, do not call round more frequently than normal (unless at the tenant's request). If the tenant makes a formal complaint about you, stop calling round altogether and make all future demands for rent in writing. You will also at this stage probably want to consider whether to start eviction proceedings – see chapter 7. If you think that the tenant is at all likely to make a claim against you for harassment, it is a good idea to keep a diary describing all contact with the tenant, giving dates and details of conversations.

Increasing the rent

If a tenant stays in a property for many years, the landlord will need to increase the rent from time to time. This can be done in one of the following ways:

For assured and assured shorthold tenancies

- By agreement with the tenant. This is usually done by granting the tenant a new fixed term agreement at a new rent. If rent is increased by agreement, it cannot be subsequently challenged by the tenant.

- Pursuant to a rent review clause in the tenancy agreement. Again, if the terms of the rent review clause are followed properly, it is unlikely that the tenant will be able to challenge the new rent as he will be deemed to have agreed to it by signing the tenancy agreement in the first place (subject to the clause not being in breach of the Unfair Contract Terms Regulations).

- By serving a notice of increase. This has to be in the prescribed form, which can be purchased from law stationers. The new rent should take effect from the beginning of a new period of the tenancy, or after a minimum period of one month for a weekly tenancy. It cannot take effect during a fixed term, only during a periodic tenancy, i.e. after the fixed term has expired. A landlord can only increase the rent by notice once a year. If a tenant is unhappy with the new proposed rent, he can refer it to the Rent Assessment Committee (see below).

  In Scotland, this must be done by serving a notice under Section 24(a) of the Housing (Scotland) Act 1988, called an AT2 notice. The tenant must be given six months' notice of the increase of rent and if the tenant is unhappy, he can refer it to a Rent Assessment Committee. Copies of the form can be obtained at www.scotland.gov.uk/housing/leaflets.

For Rent Act tenancies

Although this book has been written more for new landlords rather than Rent Act landlords (i.e. landlords of properties where tenancies pre-date 15 January 1989 in England & Wales or 2 January 1989 in Scotland), it is useful to consider Rent Act tenancies in this context. A Rent Act tenant has a right to apply to the Rent Officer to fix a 'fair rent', which is then registered and is the maximum rent the landlord is allowed to charge the tenant. The landlord can apply to have the fair rent reregistered every two years (three years in Scotland), or before this if the circumstances of the letting or the condition of the property have changed. Thus, if the property is substantially improved by the landlord, he can then apply to have the rent increased within the two-year period (three-year period in Scotland). Both parties can challenge the rent assessed by the Rent Officer by referring it to the local Rent Assessment Committee.

Prior to 1989, fair rents were notoriously low and this was a disincentive for people to let property. Since the Housing Act 1988 (or the Housing (Scotland) Act 1988), landlords have been able to let properties at a market rent and this, together with the right to recover property under the shorthold ground, has meant that there are far more rented properties around. This, in turn, has had an effect on fair rents for Rent Act tenancies, as Rent Officers are now having to take these market rents into account when fixing the fair rent. As a result of this, Rent Act fair rents have increased, in some areas substantially, although there is now a 'cap' on the increase a Rent Officer can allow. This cap does not apply to first registration of a fair rent or where improvements or repairs to a property will increase the rent by more than 15 per cent.

If you are the owner of a property which has Rent Act tenants, you should bear this in mind when applying to have the fair rent increased – it might even be worthwhile taking some professional advice on the level of rent which is now achievable. Bear in mind that although the market rent is the starting point for Rent Officers in determining fair rents, they will then make deductions; for example, if the tenant has carried out improvements, or if the property is in poor condition, or was originally let unfurnished.

If a landlord is unhappy with the rent set by the Rent Officer, he can appeal to the Rent Assessment Committee. The procedure is similar to that for assured tenancies (ATs), as set out below.

Note

The Rent Office holds a register of fair rents which is open to inspection by the public.

Challenges to the rent – the Rent Assessment Committee

In certain circumstances an assured tenant can challenge the rent and ask the Rent Assessment Committee to review it:

- For assured shorthold tenancies (ASTs) only, during the first six months of the tenancy. In Scotland, for short assured tenancies (SATs) at any time during the period of the tenancy.

- After a notice of increase of rent (see above) has been served on the tenant.

Unlike Rent Act tenancies, the tenant cannot refer the rent to the Rent Officer and his only role with ATs and ASTs is assessing rents for the purpose of Housing Benefit payments.

When a rent is referred to the Rent Assessment Committee, it will then notify the other party and both parties will be asked to make written representations. The rent can be either considered on the written representations alone or either party can request a hearing.

The application will be considered by a panel drawn from the committee's members. Panel members can either be lawyers, valuers or lay members. There is always a valuer on every committee, and the valuer will be one who has good local knowledge of the area where the property is situated. For a hearing, the panel will normally consist of three members; for considering written representations, it may be only two.

Even if there is going to be a hearing, written representations and evidence should be sent to the panel **at least seven days** before the hearing. This is because the rules require copies to be served on the other side so the panel can be given a reasonable opportunity to consider it. If evidence is provided too close to the hearing date, you will risk having the hearing adjourned, particularly if the tenant does not attend the hearing.

What the panel has to consider is (in the case of ASTs only):

1. Is there a sufficient number of dwellings let on ATs in the area for the panel to be able to do a comparison? If yes, then:

2. Is the rent significantly higher than the level of rents in the locality (i.e. more than about five to ten per cent)? If yes, then:

3. What is the market rent for this tenancy? And:

4. From what date should any new rent start?

For ATs (not shortholds), the panel only has to consider questions 3 and 4.

The following points may assist you if you have had a property referred to the Rent Assessment Committee:

- Bear in mind that the panel will always inspect the property, so make sure it is in good condition.

- The panel will not take future works into account when assessing the rent (i.e. it will not assess a higher rent because you have planned substantial improvements).

- If improvements/repairs are being done at the property, the landlord can (and should) ask the Committee to adjourn the assessment until they are completed (because the assessed rent will probably be low if the inspection takes place while works are being carried out).

- The panel will disregard the effect of any improvements made by the tenant, any deterioration in the property caused by the tenant, and the effect of any service charges for which the landlord is responsible. Thus, the tenant will not be penalised by having his rent increased because he has carried out improvements, neither can he take advantage of his own neglect of the property by being able to claim a lower rent.

- The panel cannot take the personal circumstances of either the landlord or the tenant into account – its job is to determine the market rent.

- Evidence of the rental of lettings of a similar type in the locality (e.g. in the same street) will be very useful to the panel – it will need to know the type of tenancy, its terms, the size of the property let, the rent and what is included in the letting (e.g. if it is furnished or unfurnished, and if furnished, what is included).

- The panel will take particular note of very recent lettings, bearing in mind that the market can fluctuate over a short period.

- Advertisements for rented properties in the local paper will be of limited value, as the panel will have no evidence that these properties will actually achieve a tenant at the advertised rent.

- Bear in mind that a house will achieve a higher rental value overall if let on a room-by-room basis, with each tenant having his own tenancy agreement, as opposed to being let as one property under one tenancy agreement with all tenants having joint and several liability for the whole of the rent.

Once the panel has made its decision, it will provide both parties with a decision sheet. It will also give a statement of its reasons for coming to its decision.

There is a right of appeal from the panel's decision to the High Court, and from there to the Court of Appeal. However, you can only appeal the panel's decision on the basis that it has wrongly interpreted the law, not because you disagree with the way that it has interpreted the facts. This procedure is, of course, expensive and time-consuming and it unlikely to be followed by the small landlord.

If you are unhappy with the administration of panel cases you can complain to the Parliamentary Ombudsman. However, he will not look at the actual decision reached by the panel, just the procedures that were used to reach that decision.

In Scotland, the procedure of the Rent Assessment Committees is broadly similar. Details can be obtained from the Scottish Executive website at www.scotland.gov.uk/housing/leaflets/racs-00.asp or a guide can be obtained from the RAC offices.

Repairing duties/access

All landlords have the right to obtain access to the property to inspect its condition, but, other than in cases of extreme emergency, this must not be without the tenant's knowledge and consent. Unauthorised access by the landlord may be deemed as trespass and he may also fall foul of the harassment legislation. See the discussion above at the start of this chapter regarding the covenant of quiet enjoyment.

It is important that the property is maintained in good repair throughout the tenancy (or at least those parts for which the landlord has responsibility).

If it is not, the tenant will be able to bring proceedings in the County court (or Sheriff Court in Scotland) for a court order compelling the landlord to do the repairs, or he may be entitled to do the work himself and deduct the (reasonable) cost from the rent. Note that if the tenant wishes to bring proceedings based on disrepair, he will now have to comply with the County courts Pre-Action Protocol for Housing Disrepair cases, which came into force on 8 December 2003 (this does not apply in Scotland). This sets out the procedure which the tenant has to follow before starting a court action, which includes sending a letter to the landlord providing full details of the disrepair complained of. A copy of the Protocol can be downloaded from the Court Service website at www.courtservice.gov.uk.

The tenant will also be able to use the fact of the disrepair to defend any legal proceedings the landlord may bring, for example to obtain a possession order on the grounds of rent arrears. In this case, he will not need to comply with the Pre-Action Protocol.

The tenant, if financially eligible, will be often able to get Legal Aid. If he is successful in any legal proceedings, the landlord will also normally be ordered to pay the tenant's legal costs, which could be substantial. It is important therefore that action is taken promptly if a letter regarding disrepair is received from the tenant or from his solicitor, assuming of course that the allegations are well founded.

As well as going to court, a tenant can also complain about the condition of the property to the Housing Officer in the environmental health department of his local authority, who will normally then attend and inspect the property. If it is found to be in disrepair, the local authority has the right to enforce basic standards by serving a repairs notice on the landlord. If the landlord refuses to do the work, the local authority can bring a prosecution in the local Magistrates' Court or can do the work itself and claim the cost from the landlord. Alternatively, it can obtain a demolition order.

It is important therefore that all complaints by tenants are dealt with promptly and that the property is regularly inspected and repairs carried out as necessary. However, a landlord cannot be required by a tenant to improve a property (unless it falls short of the basic standards); for example, a tenant cannot insist on normal windows being double-glazed. Also, the legislation provides that the character and prospective life-span of a property and the locality in which it is situated will affect the standard of repair required. The standard will therefore be different for quality housing in a 'good' neighbourhood, than for poor housing in a run-down district.

Tip

If a landlord has an obligation to repair or the right to enter and repair (which is usual), then he may be liable to a passer-by or an adjoining owner if damage is caused, **even if he does not know of the problem**.

HMO properties

If you are an HMO landlord, you will, in addition to the above, need to comply with the management standards (see chapter 2). This can involve quite a lot of work. For example:

- You will probably find that light bulbs will need constant replacement, as tenants often leave them on all the time. Some landlords find that it is more economical to have fluorescent lights fitted in the hallways, which are much cheaper to run if left on permanently.

- HMO tenants sometimes just dump their rubbish outside their own door rather than put it outside so the bin men can collect it. It is often simpler to put the rubbish outside yourself, and to bag it if this is necessary. If you do not, rubbish may accumulate and upset other tenants or neighbours.

- You may also have a problem with the bin men who may refuse to collect more than two bags per house, even though this house is now an HMO. It is best to tell the local authority refuse collection department that the property is now an HMO with a certain number of units, and it will tell the bin men, rather than tell the bin men yourself. You may have to tell the department a number of times before the message gets through!

You will need to inspect HMO properties more frequently than other properties, ideally at least once a week.

Housing Benefit

You will need to keep an eye on the property and inform the Benefit Office if the tenant vacates or if his circumstances change. Keep a record of when the tenant needs to reapply for benefit and make sure that he does so.

New tenancy agreements

When a fixed term comes to an end, you may wish to grant the tenant a new fixed term. It is a good idea to do this, as you can then use this as a method of increasing the rent (see 'Rent matters' above). You can also incorporate new terms in the agreement. You may wish to do this as a result of new legislation, or to protect yourself against a problem you have encountered. If you have a number of rented properties, it is a good idea to have a standard tenancy agreement which you review from time to time to take account of these matters.

Lawpack tenancy agreements are periodically reviewed and updated to take account of legislation. Landlords' associations will also periodically review their agreements. It is best, therefore, to buy new agreements rather than just photocopying an old agreement which may be out of date. For example, tenancy agreements have had to be reviewed recently to take account of the Unfair Contract Terms Regulations.

Landlords should note, however, that it is not essential to give the tenant a new form of fixed term tenancy agreement on expiry of the old one. A tenancy agreement will automatically continue on a 'periodic' basis, from month to month if rent is paid monthly, or from week to week if the rent is paid weekly, under the same terms and conditions as the original 'fixed term' tenancy. Many tenants have continued to live in their properties for years under periodic tenancies. Indeed, a periodic tenancy is sometimes preferable as it gives more flexibility; for example, if the landlord thinks he may wish to recover his property but is not sure when, or if the tenant thinks he may need to move out (e.g. if he is likely to be relocated) during the next few months. Many agents insist on providing new tenancy agreements (and of course making a charge for this service) and this often gives the impression that a new agreement is essential; however, this is not the case. In Scotland, if a new tenancy agreement is not provided, the tenancy continues on the same terms and conditions and for the same period as the original lease. It does not therefore offer the same flexibility as a periodic tenancy in England.

Note also that a landlord cannot force a tenant to sign a new agreement if he does not want to. However, under an AST, if a tenant refuses to sign, the landlord always has the option of serving a notice seeking possession and thereafter repossessing the property if the tenant refuses to sign a new agreement, for example with an increased rent. However, if the tenancy is an AT where the shorthold/notice only ground for possession is not available or a Rent Act tenancy, the tenant will often be advised not to sign a new tenancy agreement, for example if it contains more onerous terms. There is a procedure whereby landlords of ATs can change individual terms in an agreement; however, this procedure is not available to Rent Act landlords.

Tax considerations

Tax and financial matters are not considered in detail in this book and landlords are advised to seek professional advice from an accountant or refer to Lawpack's guide, *Tax Answers at a Glance*. Tax matters change annually and it is important that landlords are aware of the current regulations. However, the following comments may give some initial assistance.

A landlord must inform the Inland Revenue that he is starting a rental business no later than 6 October after the end of the relevant tax year. As the Inland Revenue can make random enquiries and/or specific enquiries of taxpayers at any time, it is essential that proper records are kept, as well as all invoices, receipts, and bank statements.

Tip

A useful guide called *Taxation of Rents* can be obtained free of charge from the Inland Revenue.

Income Tax

Income from lettings is liable to Income Tax and is assessed under Schedule A. This includes income from all rented properties, any separate charges made to tenants for hiring furniture, service charges, and receipts from any insurance policy regarding non-payment of rent. It does not, however, include deposits which are refundable to the tenant at the end of the tenancy. Nor does it include charges for any additional services such as meals or laundry, which will normally be treated as a separate trading enterprise and taxable under Schedule D. Interest on rent paid late is also assessed under Schedule D.

You are able to offset against tax, expenses incurred wholly and exclusively for the purpose of the rental business. This does not include your time, but can include wages paid to staff. It can also include interest payments on loans for the purchase of properties and/or its contents, or for repair work and all general expenses involved in running the rental business, such as advertising, Council Tax, water rates, insurance premiums, repairs, finance costs, travelling expenses, most legal expenses, etc. Be sure to keep proper records of all your expenses, and all receipts and invoices. You may also be able to offset some capital expenses by way of a capital allowance.

The outlay for providing furniture and furnishings for furnished properties is regarded as a capital expense. However, a landlord is entitled either to deduct from income a wear-and-tear allowance of ten per cent of the rent, net of Council Tax, water bills, heat and light and any similar charges which would normally be borne by the tenant, or to deduct the full costs of renewing (but not the initial cost of) individual items as and when the expenditure is incurred. But the landlord has to use the same method consistently and cannot change from year to year.

Note

If you are letting a room in your own home, there is a substantial tax allowance, currently £4,250, before tax is payable.

Capital Gains Tax

The gain on the sale of one's own home is normally exempt from this, but the gain on the sale of an investment property is taxable. If the taxpayer has been letting his own home during an absence, for example while working abroad, the exemption is not normally jeopardised.

Expenditure on capital improvements is tax deductible and there are reliefs available for expenditure incurred before 31 March 1998. However, readers are advised to consult their accountant for further details. There is also an annual exemption against capital gains, which currently is £8,500 (2005/06). Capital gains are currently taxed as if they were the top slice of a taxpayer's income for the year.

VAT

Lettings are currently exempt from VAT, unless they are holiday lettings. Holiday lettings will be treated in the same way as any other business which is subject to VAT. Your local VAT Office can advise you.

Note

Landlords should not rely on these notes alone when dealing with their tax affairs. They are intended as helpful comments only and not as a definitive guide. Tax matters change annually and it is essential that landlords obtain up-to-date professional advice to ensure that they are complying with the law.

CHAPTER 7

Problem tenants

Take action quickly

It is essential that all problems with tenants are dealt with quickly. If you ignore them, they will just get worse. It is also wise to avoid a confrontation with tenants. If they have a complaint, try to put it right immediately. If the complaint is unreasonable, negotiate with them.

A landlord says ...

'If a tenant is always complaining, he is usually working up to non-payment of rent.'

Landlord's duty to other tenants

A landlord is not generally liable for the acts of his tenants. But he may be held responsible if he introduces tenants he knows will be bad tenants into, say, a shared house. He may also be responsible to tenants for damage caused by disrepair in one of his other tenanted properties (e.g. from leaking pipes), for which he is responsible.

However, although a landlord cannot be held responsible for the acts of his bad tenants, he may feel that he owes a moral duty to his other tenants to take steps to evict the troublesome tenant, if only to prevent the other, good, tenants from leaving the property.

Gas safety

Problems may occur when a tenant refuses access to a landlord to enable him to carry out the annual gas inspection. In the event of an incident, it will be for the landlord (or his managing agent) to show that he has taken all reasonable steps to meet his legal duties (and to avoid being prosecuted and fined). A suggested procedure is as follows:

- Tell the tenant when the inspection test will take place and give a telephone number to contact if this time is inconvenient, so another appointment can be arranged.

- If no communication is received from the tenant and the inspector is not able to gain access, write a letter to the tenant explaining that a gas safety check is a legal requirement and that it is for the tenant's own safety. Give the tenant an opportunity to make another appointment or suggest a further appointment.

- If after, say, 21 days, the tenant still fails to contact you or allow access, send a further letter, reiterating the importance of the test and asking that the tenant contact you urgently to arrange an appointment within a specified period (say 14 days).

- You should not use force to gain access to the property.

- If, after three attempts, you are still unable to gain access in order to have the safety check done, contact your local Health & Safety Executive.

- Threats of violence from the tenant will justify cutting short this process.

Records (giving the date and time and any other details) should be kept of all visits to the property and copies should be kept of all correspondence sent to the tenant.

Tip

If a landlord thinks that any gas appliances are faulty and/or there is a gas escape, he should contact Transco on 0800 111 999; it has statutory rights of entry and powers of disconnection.

Harassment legislation

It is beyond the scope of this book to consider harassment legislation in detail. Essentially, the legislation provides that harassment can be both a criminal offence and entitles the tenant to bring civil proceedings for an injunction (or interdict in Scotland) and/or damages.

- **Criminal prosecutions** are normally brought by local authorities after tenants have been to them to complain. They will always write to the landlord first, however, so any correspondence received from them should be treated seriously.

- **Civil proceedings** will be brought by the tenants themselves, usually with Legal Aid. They can prove extremely expensive for landlords, because if the tenant wins, the landlord will not only have to pay damages but also the tenant's legal costs.

The following are examples of actions which will entitle tenants and/or local authorities to invoke the legislation:

- Actual physical eviction of tenants from residential property by landlords. **Eviction of tenants should only ever be done by a court bailiff (or Sheriff Officer in Scotland) pursuant to a court order.**

- Threats of, or actual, violence and/or verbal abuse.

- Removal of doors, windows, and other items from the property.

- Disconnection of services, such as gas and electricity.

- Entering the property without the tenant's consent.

- Any act which is likely to cause the tenant to give up his occupancy of the property (even if this is not the landlord's intention).

Many landlords feel extremely frustrated by this legislation, when they see the tenants living in their property without paying rent, perhaps causing damage to the property, and using it for illegal purposes. However horrendous the tenant's conduct though, the landlord must always follow the correct procedures and should **never** resort to self-help measures. There are legal remedies available to deal with tenants who behave badly, although unfortunately they do take some time. If a landlord does not follow the proper procedure, he can find it an extremely expensive exercise.

An example

A landlord lets a flat to a young lady. She only pays the first month's rent. She then starts behaving badly, she has loud parties and the neighbours complain. Her boyfriend causes a disturbance at the property on several occasions and kicks one of the doors in. The police are called in several times. The landlord goes round several times to ask for the rent. He tells her that unless she pays the rent and behaves properly she will have to go. On at least one occasion he loses his temper and shouts at her. One week he finds that she is not at the property. He continues to visit the property but she is never there. After about three weeks he suspects that she has left and uses his keys to gain entry. The house is in a dirty condition and it is obvious that no-one has been there for some time. It is full of rubbish and there is mouldy food in the kitchen. He finds some of her personal things, such as a purse with £5 in it, clothes in the wardrobe and in the chest of drawers in the bedroom, and some videos in the lounge. However, he decides that she has left, bags up all the items left in the property, and changes the locks. None of the items left being saleable, he dumps them (apart from the money in the purse which he takes against the rent arrears), redecorates the flat, and then relets it to another tenant.

Two months later he learns of a scene at the flat when the young lady tries to gain entry and is refused by the new tenant. He is subsequently served with a County court summons for damages for harassment and unlawful eviction together with a claim for compensation for her property, and a notice stating that she has been awarded Legal Aid. He loses the case and is ordered to pay compensation to the tenant, although the sum is reduced to take account of her unpaid rent and damage to the flat. He also has to pay her legal costs, which run into several thousand pounds, as well as his own solicitor's bill.

This landlord would also have been vulnerable to a prosecution for unlawful eviction.

Had the landlord followed the correct procedure and obtained a possession order, the tenant would not have been able to make any claim against him. He would have been out of pocket but the sums involved would have been far less.

Every landlord who lets property for any period of time is bound to have at least one bad tenant. All you can do is be careful in your choice of tenant, act swiftly to resolve any problems, and if the problem cannot be resolved, follow the correct legal procedures for evicting the tenant. Unfortunately, having the occasional bad tenant is just part of the job of being a landlord and when it happens to you, you just have to accept this and deal with it in a professional way.

A landlord says ...

'A tenant who is trouble at the beginning of a tenancy will continue to be trouble to the end.'

Evicting tenants

When evicting tenants, you need to have a 'ground' for eviction and to have served the proper notice on the tenant before legal proceedings are started.

Note

Unless specifically stated, this part of the book deals only with assured tenancies (ATs) under the Housing Act 1988 and the Housing (Scotland)

Act 1988. Any references to section numbers refer to sections in those Acts, as appropriate.

Grounds for possession

These are divided into mandatory grounds and discretionary grounds. It is strongly recommended that landlords only ever evict if they have mandatory grounds for possession, as this means that the judge has no alternative but to grant an order for possession. If only discretionary grounds are claimed, the tenant may be able to get Legal Aid to defend the proceedings and you will be faced with a large legal bill if you lose.

Also, if a possession order is granted under a discretionary ground the tenant has the right to ask the court to delay the actual possession date if he agrees to pay off any rent arrears by instalments, and the court will usually agree to this (even if you do not). However, under a mandatory ground, once the order is made, possession is normally ordered to be given up within 14 days, and the judge can only delay the date for possession for up to six weeks if the tenant can prove exceptional hardship.

There are several mandatory grounds for possession, but two that are most commonly used are:

- **The shorthold ground.** If a tenancy is an assured shorthold tenancy (AST) (or a short assured tenancy (SAT) in Scotland), the landlord is entitled to a possession order as of right, after the fixed term has expired, provided the proper form of notice (called a Section 21 notice) is served. In Scotland, a Section 33 notice is served along with a notice to quit which must be in the correct statutory form.

- **Serious rent arrears (Ground 8).** Provided that both at the time of service of the notice (a Section 8 notice) and at the time of the court hearing, the tenant is in arrears of rent of more than eight weeks or two months, the landlord will be entitled to possession as of right. In Scotland, the landlord needs to serve a notice to quit and an AT6 notice specifying Ground 8 and the tenant must be in arrears of more than three months.

> **Tip**
>
> When claiming under Ground 8, it is normal to also quote Grounds 10 and 11 (any rent arrears and persistent late payment of rent). These are discretionary grounds relating to rent, but they will not normally be sufficient to obtain a possession order on their own. You can also use them when claiming under another ground (e.g. Ground 1) so you can get a money judgment for any rent arrears.

The owner-occupier ground, which allows owner-occupiers to recover possession of their homes, and which is another mandatory ground, is far less common now. This is because the shorthold ground is now generally used, and because the accelerated procedure (see below) cannot now be used for this ground.

There are other mandatory grounds, but these are rarely used and are not discussed in this book.

Most tenancies are shorthold nowadays, and if a tenant proves unsatisfactory, it is best simply to serve the Section 21 notice (or a Section 33 notice and a notice to quit in Scotland) and then issue proceedings under the shorthold ground at the end of the term. If the tenant's behaviour is so serious that you cannot wait, inform the police (if appropriate) and take legal advice immediately.

Notices

Service of the correct notice (in writing) is a prerequisite for obtaining a possession order. If you cannot prove that this was done, you will not (other than in exceptional circumstances) obtain your possession order.

The correct notice to be served will depend upon the ground you are using and whether the fixed term has expired or not.

- **Shorthold ground where the fixed term has not yet ended.** Here, the notice must be for a period of at least two months and must end at or after the end of the fixed term. So, for example, for a fixed term of six months starting on 1 January, if the notice is served on 2 January, the notice period must end on or after 30 June (which means that you cannot issue proceedings until after that date). If it is served on 1 May, it must end on or after 31 July. This form of notice can be served up to and including 30 June (when it would end on or after 31 August).

In Scotland, the notice must be for at least two months prior to the end of the fixed term and a notice to quit in the prescribed statutory form must also be served at the same time.

- **Shorthold ground after the fixed term has ended.** Here, the period of the notice must be at least two months and it must end on the last day of a 'period of the tenancy'. To continue with the example above, the periodic tenancy will start on 1 July and, presuming that rent is payable monthly, the period will be from month to month and will end on the last day in the month. So if the notice is served on 5 July, it must end on 30 September. It is a good idea to add after the date for possession the words 'or at the end of the period of your tenancy which will end next after the expiration of two months from service of this notice upon you'; this will prevent the notice being invalid if you make a mistake in the date.

  In Scotland, if no notices are served the tenancy continues by 'tacit relocation' for the term of the tenancy; for example, if the tenancy agreement is for six months, the tenancy will continue for a further period of six months and notices must be served at least two months before the end of the further six-month period.

  It is very easy to get the date wrong in this situation and this can be fatal as a recent legal case has held that if the date on the possession notice is even one day wrong, the landlord will not succeed in his claim for possession. However, a landlord can guard against invalidating the form by putting the wrong date on the form in error by adding the following wording after the date for possession 'or at the end of the period of your tenancy which will end next after the expiration of two months from the service upon you of this notice'.

  Note that the forms published by Lawpack contain special wording which will prevent them from becoming invalid if the wrong expiry date is put on by mistake.

- **All other grounds.** Here the notice must be issued in the form prescribed by Section 8 of the Act, and if parts of it are missing or crossed out in error, it may be invalid. If you are serving the notice under Ground 1, it will need to be a two-month notice, if you are serving notice under Ground 8, it is a two-week notice.

In Scotland, Form AT6 is served for the period prescribed by the Housing (Scotland) Act 1988. To terminate the tenancy you must also serve a notice to quit which has a notice period of at least 40 days. For example, even if you serve an AT6 under Ground 8, which is a two-week notice, you still need to serve a notice to quit with '40 days' notice.

If you are not sure what you are doing, you should get a solicitor to draft the notice for you. It is essential that the notice is correct as otherwise you may not be granted a possession order at court.

Always keep a copy of the notice served and a record of the date and time of service of the notice, the method of service (by post, personally, through the letter box) and the name of the person who served it. It is recommended that notices are served either by handing them to the tenant personally (the best method of service) or by putting them (in an envelope addressed to the tenant) through the letter box of the property yourself. **Do not** send them by post, as it is all too easy for the tenant to say that they got lost in the post. If this happens after you have issued proceedings, there is no way that you can prove delivery by the post office, so you will have to cancel those proceedings and start again. However, if you have written proof of receipt from the tenants (e.g. if they have referred to the notice in a letter) you should be safe. I prefer not to use recorded delivery as the tenant can refuse to accept delivery, which can cause problems.

Possession proceedings

For ATs and ASTs, there are two types of possession proceedings you can use, the 'normal' proceedings and the (so called) 'accelerated' proceedings.

- **Accelerated proceedings.** These can only be used if your ground for possession is the shorthold ground. It cannot be used to claim rent arrears. It is quicker because the evidence is given by way of a written statement to the court and there is no court hearing. If successful, you will get an order for possession (normally enforceable 14 days after the order was made) and an order that the tenant pay 'fixed costs' (if you are acting in person, this will just be the court fee). From the issue of proceedings to receipt of the order for possession, these proceedings normally take between six and ten weeks assuming nothing goes wrong.

- **Normal 'fixed date' proceedings.** These involve a court hearing where you will have to attend and present your case to the judge. However, you will also normally be entitled to a money judgment for any rent arrears due at the date of the hearing, and an order that the tenant pays future rent until he vacates the property. If the rent arrears remain unpaid, you can enforce this judgment through the courts. You will also be entitled to an order for costs (if you are acting in person, this will normally be limited to the court fee and your costs of attending the hearing). In Scotland, all proceedings for possession are under the 'summary cause procedure' at the Sheriff Court, unless in addition you are seeking payment of rent arrears in excess of £1,500, in which case an ordinary action should be raised. In all cases under the summary cause procedure, a hearing is fixed.

Unless you are very certain of what you are doing, it is really best to instruct a solicitor should it become necessary to evict your tenant. Judges do not like making possession orders and will usually refuse to do so, unless a landlord has got his paperwork right. If you make a mistake, a tenant will be able to defend (often with Legal Aid) and you may end up with no possession order and an order to pay the tenant's legal costs.

Acting in person

If you do not want to use a solicitor, you will have to act in person and bring the proceedings yourself. Note that the court papers can only be signed by either the landlord himself or his solicitor. A letting agent cannot sign on behalf of a landlord, even if he has power of attorney. The court will also need to have an address for service for the claimant (i.e. the person bringing the proceedings) in England & Wales, so landlords living abroad will need to instruct solicitors to act for them.

If you decide to act in person, you will find all the necessary forms and some helpful leaflets on the Court Service website at www.courtservice.

gov.uk (or www.scotcourts.gov.uk for Scotland). They are also available from the Court Office of your local County court in England & Wales or the Sheriff Clerk's Office or local Sheriff Court in Scotland. Fill in the forms as indicated, and make sure that when you issue the proceedings you send a cheque for the court fee (currently £150) made payable to HM Paymaster General and an extra copy of the form and any attached documents, for each defendant. In Scotland, the current fee under the summary cause procedure is £39 and cheques should be made payable to the Scottish Courts Administration.

The court will issue the proceedings and serve a copy on each defendant. At the same time you will be informed of this by notice. If you are issuing normal proceedings, you will be told the date of the court hearing (in Scotland, a hearing is always fixed in summary cause proceedings); if you are using the accelerated procedure, you will be told when you can apply to the court for a possession order. If the defendant files a defence or response to your proceedings, you should be sent a copy by the court (although it is sometimes rather slow in doing this).

Make sure that you read carefully all communications you receive from the court and follow any instructions given to you. If you need to contact the court about the case, it is essential that you quote the case number, as otherwise the court staff will not be able to locate the proper file or deal with your enquiry. Remember that it takes the court some time to deal with the issue of proceedings and enquiries; do not expect a response too soon. Some courts are slower than others and some London courts, being very busy, can be particularly slow to deal with things.

If you are using the normal proceedings or if a hearing is listed for any other type of claim (e.g. if a defence is filed in a claim brought by the accelerated procedure), make sure that you arrive at court in good time (if you are late, the case may be heard without you and your claim dismissed). If you are unavoidably detained, for example if you get stuck in traffic or have an accident, try to contact the court and let it know when you will be arriving. It may then be able to delay hearing the case until you arrive. When you arrive at court you should look at the lists for that day, which you will find pinned to a notice board near the entrance. This will tell you in which court your case is being heard and the name of the judge. You should then go to the court room and (this is most important) tell the usher you have arrived. He will then make sure that you are told when the case is being heard. If you do not contact the usher, no-one will know that you are there and, again, there is a possibility that the case may be heard without you.

Standard proceedings are normally listed at half-hour intervals and several cases will be listed together. However, if you are near the end of the list, it may be some time before your case is called, so do not expect to be called immediately (in the author's experience the only times a case is called on at the time listed is when you are late). If you are in a car park where you have to pay in advance, do make sure that you pay sufficiently to cover any delays. Note that if several of the cases in the list take longer than expected, cases further down may find that they are being called up to an hour or even two hours late.

Most possession proceedings and applications are now heard 'in chambers', which means that they are heard in the judge's private room and not in an open court. The judges are District Judges and you should address them as 'Sir' or 'Ma'am' (not 'Your Honour'). In Scotland, the proceedings are held in open court and the judge is the Sheriff and should be addressed as 'Your Lordship' or 'M'Lord' or 'Your Ladyship' or 'M'Lady'.

The claimant is heard first and will have to state his case and give evidence to support his claim. For example, for a rent arrears claim, you will have to tell the court the current rent arrears. The judge will then ask the defendant (if he attends the hearing) some questions and give him an opportunity to give his case. The judge will then make his decision. He sometimes makes a little speech when doing this and if so, it is important that you make a note of what he says (in case you disagree with it and want to take legal advice later). If the judge finds in your favour, you can then ask for your costs which, if you are acting in person, will just be the court fee and your expenses for attending the hearing. If the defendant does not attend (and defendants frequently fail to attend), you will still have to give your evidence, but it is more likely that you will succeed in getting the order that you want.

After the hearing you will be sent a court order confirming what was decided by the judge. Do check this carefully as occasionally there are mistakes. If there is an error, write to the court and ask it to amend the errors.

Instructing a solicitor

If you decide to instruct a solicitor, make sure he is one who is experienced in this type of work (many are not), and that you get a firm quotation for his costs before he does any work. Make sure that this quotation is confirmed in writing. The solicitor will need:

- The tenancy agreement.

- Copies of all notices served on the tenant.

- Details of how, when, and by whom the notices were served.

- Any correspondence with the tenant, and any other notes and paperwork.

- A schedule of the rent arrears (if you are claiming unpaid rent).

- A payment on account of costs.

Tip

Make sure that the property is in good repair before issuing proceedings for serious rent arrears. If it is not, the tenant will be able to bring a counterclaim against you (often with the benefit of Legal Aid) which may prevent you from getting possession and also make you liable for an award of damages and an order to pay his legal costs.

Evicting Rent Act tenants

It is beyond the scope of this book to deal with the eviction of Rent Act tenants. If you wish to evict a Rent Act tenant, you should seek specialist legal advice. Generally, however, you are only likely to succeed if the tenant is in serious arrears of rent, or if you are able to offer him suitable alternative accommodation.

Common law tenancies

There are some tenancies which are not covered by either the Rent Act 1997 or the Housing Act 1988. These are generally tenancies of separate flats in the property where the owner himself lives, properties let at a high rent (over £25,000 per annum) or at a low rent (£1,000 per annum in Greater London or £250 per annum elsewhere), and company lets. For these tenancies you will need to serve an old-style notice to quit and then issue the standard proceedings (with a court hearing). As this type of procedure is non-standard, it is probably best to take advice from a housing solicitor before taking any action.

Squatters and licensees

If the person occupying the property does not have a tenancy, then you will be able to use another form of possession proceedings. These proceedings are much quicker than those used for tenancies and you can sometimes obtain a possession order in less than two weeks. In Scotland, you do not need to serve notices, but the court procedure can still take about two months.

However, it is not advisable for a landlord to bring this type of proceeding on his own unless he really knows what he is doing. It would be much better to instruct a reliable firm of solicitors, experienced in eviction work.

Note

A tenant cannot become a squatter simply by staying on in the property after the end of his fixed term. He will still be a tenant.

Enforcement of possession orders

Even if you have a possession order, you cannot enforce this other than through the court bailiff (or Sheriff Officer in Scotland). Do not physically evict the tenant (or occupiers) yourself! If you do, this will be a criminal offence.

The possession order (or Court Decree in Scotland) will give a date for possession. Unless specifically authorised by the court, you will have to wait until after this date before instructing the bailiffs (or Sheriff Officer in Scotland). If the tenant is still in the property at that time, you will have to complete a request form and send this, together with the court fee, to court. It will normally take some weeks for an appointment to be arranged (unless you are evicting squatters, when the bailiffs usually act quickly). The bailiff usually visits the property before fixing the appointment to discuss the eviction with the occupiers.

In Scotland, once you have the Court Decree you can instruct the Sheriff Officer to serve it on the tenant and if he has not vacated by the date given by the Sheriff Officer the Sheriff Officer can evict him. There is no need to go back to court.

When an appointment is made, you must always arrange for someone to attend with the bailiff and formally take possession from him. You should also arrange for a locksmith to be present to change the locks. In Scotland, a Sheriff Officer will attend to this.

Excluded tenancies or licences

If the letting is one of the following:

1. to a lodger in your own home;

2. a holiday let;

there is no duty on you to obtain an order for possession for the purposes of criminal law.

You must, however, tell the occupier in writing that you want him to leave and give the occupier a reasonable period of time to vacate.

However, if it is clear that the tenant is not going to vacate voluntarily, you should consult a solicitor. You may still have to issue possession proceedings, for example of the type discussed above for squatters and licensees.

Money claims

There may be times when landlords wish to claim for rent, but do not want or need to claim for possession; for example, if the tenant has already left the property, or if the tenant (or Housing Benefit) is paying rent but there are a few weeks' rent outstanding, perhaps relating to the period before Housing Benefit started. Also, the landlord will have a claim against the tenant if he has vacated the property leaving it in a poor condition, and the damage deposit is insufficient to cover the landlord's costs of putting things right.

Many landlords are also defendants in proceedings brought by tenants for the return of their damage deposit where there is a dispute about the landlords' entitlement to retain them.

Money claims should be brought in the County court and, if (as is usual) they are for sums of less than £5,000, they will be dealt with by the small claims procedure.

In Scotland, claims should be brought to the Sheriff Court; sums of up to £750 will be dealt with by the small claims procedure and sums of £750 to £1,500 by the summary cause procedure. Sums above £1,500 are dealt with under ordinary procedure.

When bringing proceedings against tenants, landlords should ensure that they have evidence to support each and every element of their claim. For claiming rent arrears they will need a detailed rent statement showing how the rent arrears accrued. Claims for interest should be kept entirely separate and should not be included in this schedule. For claims for damages, landlords will need either an estimate or an invoice for the cost of all items/work claimed. If witnesses are to be used, you will need to have a written statement of what they are going to say, which should be signed and dated. They will, however, usually still need to attend the hearing. You will also need to prepare a written statement of your own evidence.

The County court now has a special standard form of 'directions' for defended claims relating to damage deposits and damage claims. Do note that this is not applicable in Scotland.

The form, applicable only in England & Wales, reads as follows:

1   Each party shall deliver to every other party and to the Court Office copies of all documents on which he intends to rely at the hearing. These may include:

    • the tenancy agreement and any inventory;

- the rent book or other evidence of rent and other payments made by the claimant/defendant to the claimant/defendant;

- photographs;

- witness statements;

- invoices or estimates for work and goods.

2 The copies shall be delivered no later than (either a specific date or 14 days before the hearing).

3 The original documents shall be brought to the hearing.

4 The claimant/defendant shall deliver with his copy documents a list showing each item of loss or damage for which he claims the claimant/defendant ought to pay, and the amount he claims for the replacement or repair.

5 The parties shall, before the hearing date, try to agree about the nature and cost of any repairs and replacements needed, subject to the court's decision about any other issue in the case.

6 Signed statements setting out the evidence of all witnesses on whom each party intends to rely shall be prepared and included in the documents mentioned in paragraph 1. This includes the evidence of the parties themselves and of any other witness whether or not he is going to come to court to give evidence.

7 The parties should note that:

   a. in deciding the case the judge may find it helpful to have photographs showing the condition of the property;

   b. the judge may decide not to take into account a document or the evidence of a witness if no copy of that document or no copy of a statement or report by that witness has been supplied to the other parties.

For more information about practice and procedure in the Small Claims Court, readers are referred to Lawpack's *Small Claims Kit*.

CHAPTER 8

At the end of a tenancy

When does the tenancy end?

In practice, in one of the following situations:

1. at the end of the term when the tenant leaves voluntarily;

2. when the tenant vacates after service of a notice to terminate (served either by the landlord or the tenant);

3. by agreement with the landlord; or

4. when an order for possession has been made by the court.

Normally the tenant leaves voluntarily – to use legal terminology, he 'surrenders' the tenancy. A tenant cannot force the landlord to accept a surrender before the end of the term. However, landlords are advised to agree to release the tenant if there is another suitable tenant available to take over the tenancy, provided his reasonable expenses are paid. If the tenant leaves mid-way through the term, you can still claim rent from him and if he does not pay, obtain a County court judgment (or Sheriff Court Decree in Scotland), (provided you have his new address or a contact address). You will not be able to claim rent from him after you have relet the property to another tenant (apart from existing arrears).

Tip

Do not agree to accept a 'surrender' of a tenancy until any lodgers or other occupiers who are not tenants have vacated. Or make your acceptance conditional upon receiving vacant possession. Otherwise you may become bound by any agreement they had with your tenant and it will be more difficult for you to get him out.

Sometimes a tenant will just abandon a property without giving any notice. However, problems can arise when it is not certain whether a tenant has left or not. Obviously a landlord will want to relet a property as soon as possible, particularly if there are rent arrears. But a landlord must be extremely careful in these circumstances when re-entering the property, as he may be vulnerable to a charge of unlawful eviction.

You will usually be safe to repossess if:

- the fixed term has come to an end; and

- **all** the tenant's possessions have gone, particularly if the keys are left in the property.

Be very careful if the tenant has left items at the property, particularly if the term has not come to an end. The tenant may be on a long holiday, or be in hospital, or prison. If it is not absolutely clear that the tenant has vacated permanently, you should keep out of the property and obtain a possession order through the courts. See chapter 7.

Obviously you should only be considering re-entering and repossessing if the rent is in arrears. If the rent is paid up, you should not, except in the case of emergency, enter the property at all without the tenant's permission.

Be aware also that it is not unknown for tenants deliberately to entice a landlord into taking possession of a property by making it appear as if they have vacated, so that they can then bring a claim for damages for unlawful eviction.

Tip

If a tenant hands you his keys before the term has ended saying he wants to give up his tenancy, make it very clear that you do not accept his surrender, and that you will hold him responsible for the rent until another tenant is found. If you do not do this, you may be deemed to have accepted the surrender.

Handover procedure

When it is time for the tenant to go, you should arrange for an appointment with him at the property. You should then check over the contents and condition of the property with him, using the inventory and schedule of condition. Usually you should be able to decide there and then whether you will need to make any retention from the damage deposit and if so, how much this should be for. The damage deposit should then be returned to the tenant as soon as possible; however, not until after:

- the tenants have vacated the property and returned the keys; and

- you are sure that there is not going to be any claw-back from the Housing Benefit Office.

Remember, when making retentions from the damage deposit, that you must allow for fair wear and tear. The property will normally have been occupied for a long period and it is unrealistic to expect it to be in the same pristine condition that it was, at the start of the tenancy. If it is left in a dirty condition, you are entitled to claim for the reasonable costs of having the property cleaned.

Tenants often complain that landlords make deductions for damage done to the property when the damage should have come under the 'fair wear and tear' exception, and there is often some confusion as to when this should apply. An example:

- If a property is let with a rather worn carpet in the hall, and during the period of the tenancy someone's foot catches on a worn patch and it tears, this damage will come under the 'fair wear and tear' exception.

- However, if the property is provided with a brand new carpet at the start of the tenancy but when the tenant leaves this is found to have a number of cuts in it and/or large and unsightly stains which cannot be removed, then the tenant will normally be liable for the cost of a replacement carpet and the cost of this can be deducted from the damage deposit.

Make sure that you keep full records to back up any deductions made from damage deposits, for example estimates and receipts, photographs and (in bad cases) even a video to provide a record of the condition of the property after the tenant has left. Then if the tenant challenges any deductions made by you by bringing a County court claim for recovery of the damage deposit, you will have a good chance of defeating the claim. Judges do have a tendency to favour tenants in this type of claim so you need to have good evidence to prove that the expenditure was made (and that you did not simply pocket the deposit money) if this happens. You should retain this information for at least six years.

If there are arrears of rent outstanding, the damage deposit should be dealt with in the following way:

1. make deductions for damage/repairs/cleaning as appropriate; if any money is left, then

2. credit the balance against the rent arrears.

So, if there is a damage deposit of £500, damages to the value of £300 and rent arrears of £600, the £300 damages are taken first from the damage deposit leaving £200 to offset against the arrears. If you are then in a position to bring a County court claim against the tenant (i.e. if you have his new address and consider he will be worth suing), your claim will be for the balance of the rent arrears due, i.e. £400.

Tip

Do not return the damage deposit until after you have done a careful inspection of the property – once you have returned the damage deposit it is very difficult, if not impossible, to get it back.

A letting agent says ...

'We find that most problems with damage deposits are caused by landlords being unreasonable about damage due to wear and tear.'

Tenant's property left behind

This is often a great problem for landlords, because they will want to clear the property and relet it as soon as possible. But landlords must be very careful when dealing with things left behind, particularly if the rented property was abandoned by the tenant, as it is not unknown for tenants to subsequently bring a claim for damages for the alleged valuable items destroyed (the author has experience of a case where Legal Aid was granted to the claimant in similar circumstances). Remember that unless the tenant has specifically given you permission to dispose of these items, you do not have the legal right to either sell them or dump them, as they do not belong to you. However, you can move them out of the property and store them elsewhere if necessary.

The procedure for dealing with this situation is laid down in an Act called the Torts (Interference with Goods) Act 1977 (not applicable in Scotland). Under this Act, a landlord can dispose of goods left behind as follows:

1. If the landlord sends a letter by recorded delivery to the tenant stating that he intends to sell/dispose of the goods and gives the following information:

    - the name and address of the landlord (i.e. where he can be contacted regarding their collection); and

    - details of the items held;

    - the place where they are held; and

    - the date after which he intends to sell the goods (this must give the tenant a reasonable time to collect the goods - say two to four weeks).

    Make sure you keep a copy of the letter sent, and the recorded delivery slip. If you are worried that the tenant will not accept the recorded delivery, it might also be an idea to hand deliver a copy of the letter to his address, so he cannot later claim that he has not received it.

2. If the landlord does not have any address for the tenant, he can sell or dispose of the goods if he is able to show that he has made reasonable attempts to locate him. This is best done by instructing tracing agents. Many will offer a 'no-trace-no-fee' arrangement. Provided the tracing

agent's report stating that he cannot locate the tenant is kept, the landlord should be safe from a claim from the tenant if he then sells or disposes of the goods.

When disposing of the goods, it is wise to keep a record of what has been done. If there is any possibility that the tenant could bring a claim, try to get an independent witness to make a statement about the items and their condition. If the goods have any value, they should be sold at the best price obtainable. Keep full records of what was done and the prices obtained.

If any of the goods are sold, the proceedings of sale are strictly speaking the property of the tenant and should be kept for him. However, the landlord is entitled to deduct the costs of sale, and if there are rent arrears outstanding or other monies due to the landlord, there is no reason why these should not also be deducted.

Death of a tenant

What happens if an assured tenancy or an assured shorthold tenancy tenant dies? If he is one of joint tenants, the tenancy will simply continue in the name of the other joint tenant/s. If the tenant is a sole tenant, then, as discussed in chapter 1, the tenancy will normally pass to the tenant's spouse or to a member of his family. If the tenancy passes to anyone other than the tenant's spouse, then the landlord has a mandatory ground for possession, provided proceedings are issued within 12 months of the tenant's death.

If the tenancy is a Rent Act tenancy, then the tenancy will pass as above to the spouse, family member, etc. The succession rights of tenants are stronger under Rent Act tenancies and there is no mandatory ground for possession.

It is beyond the scope of this book to consider the succession rights of tenants in detail. Landlords are advised to seek further advice from a solicitor, particularly if the tenant is a Rent Act tenant. For the position in Scotland, seek advice from a solicitor.

After the tenant has gone

Utilities

Make sure that a meter reading is done before the property is relet.

Post

If you do not have a forwarding address for the old tenant, do not keep or throw post away; return everything, marked 'gone away'.

You will then have to clean the property, redecorate it if necessary, and start all over again!

Tip

Try to obtain a forwarding address for the tenants. You may need it later if you have a claim against them.

Appendix

Useful addresses

Association of Residential Letting Agents (ARLA)

ARLA Administration
Maple House
53–55 Woodside Road
Amersham
Bucks HP6 6AA

Tel: 0845 345 5752
Website: www.arla.co.uk

Clerk to the Rent Assessment Committee

Sixth Floor
78 St Vincent Street
Glasgow G2 5UB

Tel: 0141 204 2261
Website: www.scotland.gov.uk/
housing

or

48 Manor Place
Edinburgh EH3 7EH

Tel: 0131 226 1123

Companies House

Crown Way
Maindy
Cardiff CF14 3UZ

Tel: 0870 333 3636
Website: www.companieshouse.
gov.uk

CORGI

1 Elmwood	Tel: 0870 401 2300
Chineham Business Park	Website: www.corgi-gas.com
Crockford Lane	
Basingstoke	
Hampshire RG24 8WG	

Health & Safety Executive

HSE Infoline: 0845 345 0055	Website: www.hse.gov.uk

Independent Housing Ombudsman Limited

Norman House, 105–109 Strand	Tel: 020 7836 3630
London WC2R 0AA	Website: www.ihos.org.uk

Inland Revenue Stamp Duty Land Tax Helpline

Tel: 0845 603 0135
Website: www.inlandrevenue.gov.uk/so

National Federation of Residential Landlords

Executive Office	Tel: 0845 4560357
PO Box 11107	Website: www.nfrl.org.uk
London SW15 6ZE	

National Inspection Council for Electrical Installation Contracting (NICEIC)

Vintage House	Tel: 020 7564 2323
37 Albert Embankment	Website: www.niceic.org.uk
London SE1 7UJ	

National Landlords Association

78 Tachbrook Street	Tel: 020 7828 2445
London SW1V 2NA	Website: www.landlords.org.uk

Office of Fair Trading

Fleetbank House	Tel: 08457 22 44 99
2–6 Salisbury Square	
London EC4Y 8JX	

Parliamentary Ombudsman

Office of the Parliamentary Commissioner for Administration Millbank Tower Millbank London SW1P 4QP	Tel: 0845 015 4033

For *unfair contract terms* contact:

The Business Support Team
Tel: 020 7211 8948
Website: www.oft.gov.uk

Rent Service

Fourth Floor 5 Welbeck Street London W1G 9YQ	Tel: 020 7023 6000 Website: www.therentservice. gov.uk

Royal Institution of Chartered Surveyors (RICS)

RICS Contact Centre Surveyor Court Westwood Way Coventry CV4 8JE	Tel: 0870 333 1600 Website: www.rics.org.uk

Transco

Tel: 0800 111 999

CORGI – Confederation for the Registration of Gas Installers

By law, anyone carrying out gas-related work must be CORGI-registered. To comply with the Gas Safety Regulations, landlords must ensure that the person who does the safety checks and any work is CORGI-registered, and is also registered to do the type of work required.

CORGI-registered installers have to undergo rigorous training and regular retraining and inspection before they obtain their competency certificates. Every registered CORGI installer must have a CORGI ID card. You should ask to see this before any work is done. Their registration is limited to the types of work they are qualified to do, details of which are set out on the reverse of their ID card.

If you are unhappy about the standard of work done by a CORGI-registered installer, CORGI will often agree to inspect this free of charge, as part of its monitoring programme. It can be contacted on 0870 401 2300.

CORGI has an excellent website at www.corgi-gas-safety.com. There are facilities online to find a registered installer or to check that an installer is registered.

Index

A

'accelerated' proceedings 109-10

access agreements 3-4, 75, 76, 88, 94-6, 102-3

accreditation for landlords 43

addresses

    for landlords 77-8

    for tenants 123, 125

administration expenses 71

advertising

    of properties 49, 94

    for tenants 48-9

agents

    letting agents 45-8

    tracing agents 123-4

alterations, to properties 75 *see also* building work; repairs

Antisocial Behaviour, Etc. (Scotland) Act 2004 13

antisocial tenants 13, 49-50, 101-2, 104-5

assignment 76

associations, landlord ix, 26-7, 46

ASTs (assured shorthold tenancies) 4, 8-9

    eviction *see* eviction

    renewal 98

    rent 90, 92-3

    terms *see* terms

    written, verbal and 63-4

asylum seekers 53

AT2 notices 90

AT5 notices 9

ATs (assured tenancies) 4, 9
   eviction *see* eviction
   renewal 98
   rent 90, 93
   see also ASTs

B
bailiffs 114-15
beginning of tenancies 66-7
belongings, left by tenants 77, 104-5, 123-4
Benefit, Housing *see* Housing Benefit
building work 17-18
   regulations 30, 32
   see also alterations, to properties; repairs
buy-to-let properties 15, 20-2

C
Capital Gains Tax 99-100
city properties 16, 17
claw-back, Housing Benefit 57-8
common law tenancies 113-14
company lets 5, 52, 114
condensation problems 32-3
considerate tenants 49, 50-1
contact details
   for landlords 77-8
   for tenants 123, 125
CORGI-registered work 33, 34, 130
corporate tenants 48
Council Tax 42, 69
country properties 16-17
County court 95, 116
Court Decrees 114, 115, 119
covenant of quiet enjoyment 87-8
credit reference agencies 51-2

D
damage to properties 50, 75
death, of tenants, succession 12, 124

defaulters 19-20
deposits 71-3, 121-2
descriptions, of properties 49, 69
disruptive tenants 13, 49-50, 101-2, 104-5
duration of tenancies 66-7 *see also* fixed-term tenancies; periodic tenancies

E

electrical equipment, regulations 35, 38-9
Electrical Equipment (Safety) Regulations 1994 38-9
electrical systems 35, 96
employee lettings 7
end of tenancies
    eviction *see* eviction
    handover 121-2
    scope 119
    surrender 2, 119, 120-1
eviction 12
    acting in person 110-12
    forfeiture 78-9
    grounds 106-9
    limitations 110
    notice 107-9
    repossession from 109-13, 114-15, 120
    scope 113-15
    unlawful 103, 104-5, 120
    see also surrender
expenses 45, 71, 99, 100

F

farms, agricultural restrictions 30
fees
    for administration 71
    for letting agents 45
fire safety
    furnishings 38
    precautions 35-6
fittings 18, 37
fixed-term tenancies 9-10, 67-8
    eviction 108

renewal 97
forfeiture 78-9
furnished properties 19
furnishings 18-19, 37
   fire safety 38
Furniture and Furnishings (Fire) (Safety) Regulations 1988 38

G
garages 69
gardening 75
Gas Safety (Installation and Use) Regulations 1998 33
gas systems
   inspections 102-3, 130
   precautions 33, 34, 130
   problems 33-4
General Product Safety Regulations 1994 39
good tenants 49, 50-1
grants, for refurbishment 18, 31-2
guarantees, of rent 10-11, 82
   safeguarding 53
gut feelings, on tenants 51, 52-3

H
harassment 80, 87-8, 103-5
   rent collection and 89
Health & Safety Executive (HSE) 34
heating systems 32, 79
HMOs (houses in multiple occupation) 6
   Housing Benefit 56
   limitations 23-4, 25
   regulations 24-5, 96-7
   scope 22-3
holiday lets 6, 15, 16-17
   eviction 115
   as residential lettings 80
homeless tenants 53
homes, letting one's own 11-12, 15
houses in multiple occupation *see* HMOs
Housing Act 1996 3, 10

Housing Act 2004 6, 13, 22, 23, 73
Housing Acts 1988 3, 4, 5, 10, 78, 91
Housing Benefit 59, 97
   applications 55-7
   claw-back 57-8
   houses in multiple occupation 56
   letters of authority 54, 55
   Local Housing Allowance 58
   scope 55
   unit calculations 56
   valuations 60-1
Housing Benefit Office 57, 59
Housing (Scotland) Act 1987 31
HSE (Health & Safety Executive) 34

I
Income Tax 99
information packs, for new tenants 81
inherited properties 15
Inland Revenue 98
instinct, on tenants 51, 52-3
insurance 40-2, 77
internet, for tenants 49
inventories 39-40, 81

J
judges 112

K
keyholders 36, 120-1

L
Landlord and Tenant Act 1985 31
Landlord and Tenant Act 1987 77
landlords xi *see also individual terms*
landlords' associations ix, 26-7, 46
Law Commission 13
legislation 1, 3, 13 *see also individual terms*
letters of authority 54, 55

letting agents 45-8
liability, joint and several, for rent 11
licences 2, 88
   employee lettings 7
   holiday lets 6, 15, 16-17, 80, 115
   houses in multiple occupation *see* HMOs
   lodgers 6, 115
   as written 64
licensees, eviction 114
lighting 96
local authorities 23, 25-6, 60, 95, 96, 103-4
Local Housing Allowance 58
location factors 16-17
locks 36
lodgers 6
   eviction 115

M
management contracts 46-7, 96
money claims 115-17
mortgages 20

N
National Federation of Residential Landlords (NFRL) ix, 27
newsagents, for tenants 48
NFRL (National Federation of Residential Landlords) ix, 27
noise abatement 87
'normal' proceedings 110, 111-12
notice boards, for tenants 48

O
occupancy limits 30
Office of Fair Trading (OFT) 64
outbuildings 69

P
payments by tenants 69-70
   deposits 71-3, 121-2

premiums 12
  rent *see* rent
penalty clauses 70-1
periodic tenancies 9
  eviction 108
  renewal 97-8
permission
  to let 29
  planning 29-30
pets 79
Planning Officers 30
planning permission 29-30
Plugs and Sockets, Etc. (Safety) Regulations 1994 39
possession orders 106-9
possessions, left by tenants 77, 104-5, 123-4
post
  for landlords 77-8
  for tenants 109, 123, 125
power of attorney 47
Pre-Action Protocol for Housing Disrepair 1993 95
premiums 12
press, for tenants 48
privacy rights, of tenants 87, 88
Property Misdescriptions Act 1991 49

R
references
  financial 51-2
  instinct and 51
  personal 51
  professional 51
refuse collection 96
renovation 30-2, 74-5, 88, 94-6 *see also* alterations, to properties;
building work
rent 2, 5-6, 10-11, 53, 82
  books for 89
  challenges 90-1, 92-4
  claims 115-17

collection 68-9, 89, 119
composition 42, 70
   on deposits 122
due dates 67, 68
as fair 90-1
high 5-6
Housing Benefit on *see* Housing Benefit
increases 89-91
late 70
low 5-6
reviews 74
setting 19, 42
unpaid 71, 106-7
Rent Act 1977 2, 5
Rent Act (Scotland) 1984 5
Rent Act tenancies 5
   death and 124
   eviction 113
   rent 90-1
Rent Assessment Committees 90, 92-4
rent books 89
Rent Officers 56, 60, 61, 91
rent reviews 74
Rent Service 59, 60, 61
repairs 30-2, 74-5, 88, 94-6 *see also* alterations, to properties; building work
repossession 109-13, 114-15, 120
resident landlords 7-8

S
safety precautions 38-40 *see also individual terms*
SATs (short assured tenancies) 4, 9
schedules of condition 39-40, 81
SDLT (Stamp Duty Land Tax) 12, 82
seasonal demands 80
second homes, letting 15
security of tenure 2
Sheriff Court 95, 116

Sheriff Officers 114-15
Sheriffs 112
short assured tenancies (SATs) 4, 9
solicitors 113
squatters 2
   eviction 114
Stamp Duty Land Tax (SDLT) 12, 82
subletting 76
succession 12, 124
surrender 2, 119, 120 *see also* eviction

T

tax 98
   Capital Gains Tax 99-100
   Council Tax 42, 69
   expenses on 45, 71, 99, 100
   Income Tax 99
   Stamp Duty Land Tax 12, 82
   VAT 100
tenancy agreement forms 82-3, 84-5
   renewal 97-8
tenants 17, 41 *see also individual terms*
terms 82
   essential 66-9
   as fair 64-6, 79-80
   fixed 9-10, 67-8, 97, 108
   optional 69-82
   periodic 9, 97-8, 108
   written, verbal and 63-4
Torts (Interference with Goods) Act 1977 123-4
tracing agents 123-4
Trading Standards Office 40

U

Unfair Terms in Consumer Contracts Regulations 1999 64-5
unfurnished properties 19
universities, for tenants 48
use of property 75

V
VAT 100
ventilation problems 33-4

W
water 37, 69-70

MORE BOOKS AVAILABLE FROM LAWPACK

MORE BOOKS AVAILABLE FROM LAWPACK

Buying Bargains at Property Auctions

Every week, hundreds of commercial and residential properties are sold at auction in Britain, often at bargain prices, with owner-occupiers accounting for a growing proportion of buyers. In this bestselling guide, author and property auctioneer Howard Gooddie spells out how straightforward the auction route can be and divulges the tips and practices of this relatively unknown world.

Code B626 | ISBN 1 904053 89 0 | Paperback | 153 x 234mm | 304pp | £11.99 | 4th edition

The Buy-to-Let Bible

Low mortgage rates and under-performance by traditional savings and investment products means that property has never looked a better way to invest for the future. Author Ajay Ahuja divulges the practical and financial techniques that have made him a millionaire. It covers finding the right property, the right mortgage lender, the right tenant, legal issues and tax.

Code B637 | ISBN 1 904053 91 2 | Paperback | 153 x 234mm | 256pp | £11.99 | 3rd edition

The Seven Pillars of Buy-to-Let Wisdom

In his first, bestselling buy-to-let book, *The Buy-to-Let Bible* author and buy-to-let millionaire Ajay Ahuja provided the basics of successful buy-to-let. Ajay has now written 'further reading' for the buy-to-let investor, *The Seven Pillars of Buy-to-let Wisdom*, that explains in depth how to get the most from your investment by examining the seven fundamentals of successful buy-to-let property management.

Code B447 | ISBN 1 904053 42 4 | Paperback | 153 x 234mm | 144pp | £9.99 | 1st edition

To order, visit **www.lawpack.co.uk** or call **020 7394 4040**

MORE BOOKS AVAILABLE FROM LAWPACK

Book-Keeping Made Easy

This guide provides the new business owner with an understanding of the fundamental principles of book-keeping, showing how to set up accounts and how to benefit from the information they contain. Includes procedures for the sole proprietor and small business, accounting for growing businesses, double-entry book-keeping, ledgers, payroll and final accounts.

Code B516 | ISBN 1 904053 85 8 | Paperback | 153 x 234mm | 104pp | £10.99 | 2nd edition

Business Agreements Made Easy

This book's primary focus is business-to-business contracts for supply of services and/or goods with limited reference to business-to-consumer contracts. It explains the key commercial and legal issues which occur throughout a 'contract lifecycle' (i.e. from pre-contract stage to negotiation of contract to end of contract) with suggested actions and steps.

Code B519 | ISBN 1 904053 84 X | Paperback | 153 x 234mm | 144pp | £11.99 | 1st edition

Business Letters Made Easy

Business Letters Made Easy provides an invaluable source of 199 ready-drafted letters for a range of business situations. Each letter has a useful commentary, explaining when to use a particular letter and helping you choose the right turn of phrase. This book takes the headache and time-wasting out of letter writing, and provides you with letters that get results!

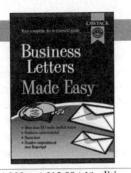

Code B520 | ISBN 1 904053 87 4 | Paperback | 153 x 234mm | 288pp | £12.99 | 1st edition

To order, visit **www.lawpack.co.uk** or call **020 7394 4040**

MORE BOOKS AVAILABLE FROM LAWPACK

101 Ways to Pay Less Tax

This book provides a wealth of tax saving tips from H M Williams Chartered Accountants, a national award winning firm of chartered accountants.

The tips included in this book are all legitimate ways to help reduce your tax bill – tax avoidance rather than tax evasion.

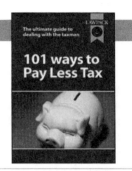

Code B448 | ISBN 1 904053 71 8 | Paperback | 153 x 234mm | 184pp | £9.99 | 1st edition

Proper Coffee

Management tomes abound but they can be turgid to wade through. This book provides a refreshing alternative for the small business. It provides succinct, practical advice on how to raise the bottom line and increase profitability, without working any harder.

Code B451 | ISBN 1 904053 86 6 | Paperback | 153 x 234mm | 150pp | £9.99 | 1st edition

Tax Answers at a Glance 2005/06

We all need to get to grips with the array of taxes now levied by the government. Compiled by award-winning tax experts and presented in question-and-answer format, this handbook provides a useful and digestible summary of Income Tax, Capital Gains Tax, Inheritance Tax, pensions, self-employment, partnerships, Corporation Tax, Stamp Duty/Land Tax, VAT, and more.

Code B625 | ISBN 1 904053 76 9 | Paperback | 153 x 234mm | 208pp | £9.99 | 5th edition

To order, visit **www.lawpack.co.uk** or call **020 7394 4040**

MORE BOOKS AVAILABLE FROM LAWPACK

301 Legal Forms, Letters & Agreements

Our best-selling form book is now in its eighth edition. It is packed with forms, letters and agreements for legal protection in many situations. It provides a complete do-it-yourself library of 301 ready-to-use legal documents, for business or personal use. Areas covered include loans and borrowing, buying and selling, employment, transfers and assignments and residential tenancy.

Code B402 I ISBN 1 904053 66 1 I Paperback I A4 I 384pp I £19.99 I 8th edition

Personnel Manager

A book of more than 200 do-it-yourself forms, contracts and letters to help your business manage its personnel records. Areas covered include recruitment and hiring, employment contracts and agreements, handling new employees, personnel management, performance evaluation and termination of employment.

Code B417 I ISBN 1 904053 23 8 I Paperback I A4 I 272pp I £14.99 I 3rd edition

Ready-Made Company Minutes & Resolutions

Maintaining good, up-to-date records of company meetings and resolutions is not only good practice but also a legal requirement, whatever size your company is. This book of forms makes compiling minutes of board and shareholder meetings straightforward. It includes more than 125 commonly-required resolutions and minutes to save you time and effort.

Code B616 I ISBN 1 904053 73 4 I Paperback I A4 I 192pp I £14.99 I 3rd edition

To order, visit **www.lawpack.co.uk** or call **020 7394 4040**

Visit the new Lawpack website and order online at www.lawpack.co.uk

What's new?

We've tried to retain the ease of use of our old site, while offering much more in terms of free legal information, more comprehensive product descriptions to give a true idea of what you're buying and links to qualified solicitors and legal resources if our products aren't appropriate for your situation.

Comprehensive product listings

First and foremost, Lawpack is a DIY legal publisher, and our ever-expanding range of easy-to-use titles is brought to life on the new website with extensive product overviews, author biographies, full content details and recommendations of other complementary titles in our range.